ROCK en Español

The Latin Alternative Rock Explosion

Ernesto Lechner

CHICAGO REVIEW PRESS

An A Cappella book

I dedicate this book to the memory of my brother
Sebastián Alejandro Lechner (1959–1999). It was thanks
to him that I listened to the rebellious sounds of rock en
español for the first time in our Buenos Aires home.

Siempre estás conmigo, mijenlis.
Esto es para vos.

Library of Congress Cataloging-in-Publication Data
Lechner, Ernesto.
    Rock en Español : the Latin alternative rock explosion / Ernesto
Lechner.— 1st ed.
        p. cm.
    Includes discography (p. 247).
    ISBN-13: 978-1-55652-603-9
    ISBN-10: 1-55652-603-2
    1. Alternative rock musicians—Latin America. 2. Alternative
rock musicians—Spain. 3. Alternative rock music—Latin America—
History and criticism. 4. Alternative rock music—Spain—History
and criticism. I. Title.
    ML394.L37 2005
    781.66098—dc22

                                        2005030183

Cover and interior design: Scott Rattray
All photos ©Maria Madrigal/*La Banda Elástica* unless otherwise noted.

*Parts of this book have previously appeared in a different form as
articles written for the* Los Angeles Times, *the* LA Weekly, *the*
Chicago Tribune, *and* the Grammys.

Published by Chicago Review Press, Incorporated
814 North Franklin Street
Chicago, Illinois 60610
ISBN-13: 978-1-55652-603-9
ISBN-10: 1-55652-603-2
Printed in the United States of America
5 4 3 2 1

Contents

Acknowledgments

I AM FOREVER indebted to the following people for putting up with me while I wrote this book: Sandra (*mi negrita*), Claudia Andrea (*mi princesa*), and Sebastián Ernesto (*mi pequeño zorro*). Also to Enrique Lechner, Alicia Renard, Andrea Lechner, Amadeo Lechner, Vivi Lechner, Claudia Bautista Nicholas, Atilio Pernisco (*gracias, vieja*), and Rudy Regalado. A million thanks to Valeria Agis, Walter Ziffer, and Patricia Flores for standing by me when the going got tough.

Many thanks to the Latin rock community for making me believe that I knew enough about *rock en español* to write a book about it. In particular, Emilio Morales and María Madrigal (*La Banda Elástica*), Enrique Lopetegui, Josh Norek, Tomás Cookman, Josh Kun, Gustavo Santaolalla, Aníbal Kerpel, and everyone at Surco.

To all the wonderful editors whose guidance helped me become a better writer: Robert Hilburn, Richard Cromelin, Randy Lewis, Lee Margulies, and Rich Nordwind at the *Los Angeles Times*; Scott Powers, Heidi Stevens, and Kevin Williams at the *Chicago Tribune*; Sandra Guzman at the *New York Post*; Nathan Brackett at *Rolling Stone*; Serena Kim at *Vibe*; Ray Rogers at *Interview*; Peter Melton at *Pulse!*; John Payne at the *LA Weekly*; Phil Gallo at *Variety*; Lourdes Centeno at *People en Español*; Antonio Mejías, Juan Rodríguez Flores, and Hugo Quintana at *La Opinión*; and last but not least, David Konjoyan at the Grammys for his constant encouragement.

To Dan Mandel and Yuval Taylor for their undying enthusiasm.

Finally, to all the artists mentioned in this book, particularly Julieta Venegas and Saúl Hernández for their unbelievable generosity.

Foreword
by Saúl Hernández of Jaguares

Mexico City

It was seven P.M. and I was standing by the Insurgentes metro station with Pepe Navarro and Salvador de la Fuente. We were Deimos, my first band. That night would change my life.

Mistus was performing and La Caja de Pandora was opening for them. But La Caja de Pandora faded away in the boulevards of Mexico City, swallowed by fate and distance. They never showed up.

I don't remember exactly how it happened, but somebody (it was El Bola, I know now) approached us and asked if we were a band and would we care to perform that night. I had never seen so many people together sharing that special vibe that you find at concerts—the sense of communion, a ceremonial ritual. It was my initiation, my baptism, my road. I was fifteen years old.

It was the seventies, an era that changed our destiny. A time of intolerance and repression. The abuse of power threw us into an abyss from which many of us would never be able to emerge. We found a refuge there, a unique corner where it was just ourselves and our loneliness. A space forgotten by society and protected by angels. It taught us that marginalization has its own powerful side, covered with light, possessing what the other side lacks: dignity. That smelly gutter would be our home, and repression our mentor. It was there that survival developed its own world, an intimate language, a heartrending scream that fought for the right to exist.

Music, the eternal friend, forges ahead, and I do not know where it will take me. It's 2005: a new century, new sounds, the same search.

I believe all of the bands that make up this book and the history of music in Spain and Latin America are engaged in the same quest. We're all looking for hope.

Like the most powerful hurricane, we will continue traveling, denouncing everything that hurts and kills us. By screaming and spitting in the face of the system we will rescue all that is lost. Reflecting spilled philosophies, seductive rhythms, and wounded melodies, we will try to touch your soul. What for? To wake you up. Better wounded than asleep, like Oliverio Girondo said.

Ernesto gives us the testimony of groups that have been witnesses and protagonists of our times. Groups that form the evolutionary chain of a musical genre that for generations has learned to survive the rotten system that surrounds us.

Ernesto's patience and dedication are valuable. Like a fallen angel, he has separated heaven from hell.

Carnales [buddies]: "Gimme Shelter" and "Let It Be."

Saúl
August 2005

Introduction

I WAS INTRODUCED to the beauty of Latin rock against my will.

In 1997, I was hired by the *Los Angeles Times* as a freelance Latin music critic. I was responsible for delivering a somewhat objective view of the music's many genres—from regional Mexican and salsa to Brazilian and rock. I had been a devoted fan of Brazilian music all my life and had become addicted to the Afro-Caribbean tinge while living in Los Angeles. My feelings for our own brand of rock, however, were a different story.

Growing up in Argentina, I was very much familiar with the efforts of the last three and a half decades to transpose the roots of rock 'n' roll into a vernacular musical idiom. To be honest, I didn't think that the resulting music was very good at all. To me, *rock en español* was all about aping the much better stuff that was being made in England and the United States. How could Soda Stereo or Caifanes compare with the Beatles, the Rolling Stones, Pink Floyd, Velvet Underground, or the Cure? The concept of *"rock en español"* itself seemed ludicrous to me. Rock in Spanish? Why? I was too busy listening to Led Zeppelin, U2, and Marvin Gaye.

Time after time, I have returned to the old Latin rock records of the sixties, seventies, and eighties. I always find enjoyable elements in them. But the vintage efforts by Sui

Géneris, El Tri, and Soda Stereo are firmly rooted in a specific era—and time has only exposed the sonic limitations of the equipment with which they were recorded.

But then something happened.

As it turns out, the late nineties was a time of tremendous growth and transformation for Latin rock—and I happened to be there, and to be given a reporter's full access to the unfolding movement. This moment was all about the blossoming of a new generation of bands who were turning Latin alternative into one of the decade's most exciting movements in the world. The young musicians, producers, and composers were not content anymore with simply emulating whatever musical format was trendy up North—protest songs in the sixties, prog-rock in the seventies, and new wave in the eighties. Sure, the sounds of rock, punk, hip-hop, and electronica were present in their work, but there was also the refreshing appearance of a new element. These musicians had grown up listening to their parents' record collection of Latin American popular music: boleros, bossa nova, salsa, cumbias, and syrupy Latin pop.

The influence was inescapable. Latin rock came of age by blending foreign influence with local roots. The result was—and still is—irresistible.

The transformation had already begun in the late eighties through groups such as Spain's Mano Negra and Argentina's Fabulosos Cadillacs. During the late nineties and the beginning of the millennium, all of the movement's major players released the best albums of their career.

I was lucky to be there, and a few pivotal events made me fall irreparably in love with Latin rock: the recording sessions of Mexican quartet Café Tacvba's masterful *Revés/Yosoy*; the electrifying shows that Colombia's Aterciopelados presented in conjunction with the release of their ode to trip-hop *Caribe atómico*; meeting Mexico's Julieta Venegas and experiencing the melancholy textures of her *Bueninvento* album; the carnivalesque shows that Fabulosos Cadillacs presented in Los Angeles; and, in 2004, the appearance of *Infame*, the lounge-rock masterpiece by Argentina's Babasónicos.

Interestingly, as *rock en español* grew in stature and quality, so-called mainstream rock began a slow and painful descent into mediocrity. Soon enough, listening to El Gran Silencio and the Nortec Collective became much more fascinating to me than following the careers of Björk or Massive Attack.

This book is the result of eight years of nonstop listening to and exploring this vibrant genre. The intention is not to deliver a definitive history of Latin rock, but rather to provide fans and genre neophytes alike with a little bit of insight, information, and suggestions for further listening. I hope this book will make you disagree with many of my views—or perhaps even agree with a few of them. *Rock en español* has so much life and magic in it that a conversation on its history and merits is by necessity a dialogue filled with contradictory opinions and perhaps some exaggeration as well.

I have included separate chapters on the nineteen artists whose music has moved me to write about them—not because I was assigned a story on them, but because I felt a fan's desire to understand what their creations are all about.

Nineteen artists are hardly enough to cover a movement that includes musicians from so many different countries. At the end of the book you will find an appendix with short entries on the dozens of other Latin rockers who I believe are indispensable for the understanding of the genre. I've also included a list of the top one hundred Latin albums that are necessary for any collection.

I am particularly proud of the fact that this book spends very little time on so-called Latin rock artists such as Shakira or Maná. Any *rock en español* fan worth his salt will tell you that neither of them belongs in the defiantly unique aesthetic of the movement. Better not debate the relative artistic merit of an artist like Shakira—her arena shows are undeniably lots of fun—but rather concentrate on the bands and solo artists who have made a serious contribution to Latin alternative as an innovative field.

Right after Ricky Martin ignited the "Latin Music Explosion" in 1999, Latin labels operating in the United States thought of Latin rock as a genre with tremendous crossover potential. A lot of money was spent and coordinated efforts were made to convince American consumers that Café Tacvba's *Revés/Yosoy* (ironically, their most blatantly experimental album) and Aterciopelados' *Gozo poderoso* were destined for the *Billboard* charts. Fortunately (or unfortunately, depending on your point of view) those efforts went nowhere fast. *Rock en español* is too idiosyncratic a musical expression for massive consumption in the English-speaking world. True, many of the genre's best bands are still starving as a result of this, but at least their artistic vision is generally not compromised. Selling out stadiums in Latin America isn't that bad, either, and many of the bands mentioned in this book are superstars in their respective countries.

Like every music critic I have ever met, I began writing about records motivated by my desire to share with others the sounds that I feel so passionate about. I am still amazed at the ability of music—and Latin rock in particular—to bring together people of different cultures, nations, and ethnic backgrounds.

Que viva el rock.

Ernesto Lechner
Los Angeles, June 2005

Fabulosos Cadillacs

IT'S A BLISTERING Los Angeles afternoon in the summer of 1998, and the members of Latin rock supergroup Fabulosos Cadillacs are definitely not thrilled to be meeting with me.

We're at the entrance of a Hollywood television studio where the band is taping an appearance on *Vibe*. They're on tour in the United States—a country for which they have often expressed a visceral dislike. So they're in a bad mood, their behavior bordering on rudeness when I introduce the photographer who has come along with me to take pictures for a *Los Angeles Times* Sunday profile.

She suggests a photo next to an American flag that stands on the corner of the soundstage. The shot could symbolize the Cadillacs' success in the United States.

"Absolutely not," barks bassist and co-leader Flavio Cianciarulo. He is a chunky man with an unkempt beard, his strong arms covered with colorful tattoos.

Singer Gaby Fernández Capello, better known as Vicentico, doesn't look as threatening as Cianciarulo, but a sarcastic smirk denotes his total indifference for the trappings of success that so many other performers are quick to embrace. If it were up to him, there would probably be no interviews with the media at all. "Look, *boludo*," he tells Cianciarulo with a snicker, knowing that the middle-aged photographer from the *Times* doesn't speak Spanish. "They sent an old lady so that we wouldn't have the nerve to beat her up."

I look at them while the photographer patiently instructs them to stand by the entrance of the stage, where the lighting is good, and I sigh. How can these two creeps who look like they haven't showered in days be responsible for some of the most astonishing and heartfelt music in the history of Latin American rock? If there's one band responsible for taking *rock en español* out of an aesthetic ghetto of sorts and imbuing it with unsuspected creativity and depth, the Cadillacs are it. It is no coincidence that a few months ago *Fabulosos calavera* (Fabulous Skull) won the first Grammy ever awarded for a Latin rock record. Even seven years later, it will still stand as the Latin American equivalent of the Beatles' *Sgt. Pepper's Lonely Hearts Club Band.*

"One more over here," says the photographer tersely.

"I'm gonna kill her," retorts Vicentico in Spanish.

Fortunately, the Cadillacs' manager politely interrupts the photo session. The band needs to go onstage for a quick rehearsal.

I follow them onto the *Vibe* stage, and see the full group ready to perform "Surfer calavera," the one song in the album that the Cadillacs' record label is desperately trying to push as a possible hit single—under the false hope that the band will be able to recapture the glories of "Matador," the phenomenal, batucada-flavored smash that turned the group into a worldwide sensation back in 1994.

As a completely uninterested Vicentico positions himself in front of the mike and waits for his vocal cue, the rest of the group performs the intro, a retro-sounding bit of crackling drums, R&B brass, and wah-wah guitars. A falsetto chorus is heard, as well as the rugged voice of Cianciarulo murmuring something about a skeleton surfing under the silvery moon on the waters of Mar del Plata, the popular seaside resort in Argentina where he was born.

The band pauses for a moment, then launches into a deafening call-and-response chorus that's equal parts thrash metal and Saturday morning cartoon music. Cianciarulo cackles while Vicentico sings of Death, which is seen throughout the

new album as a buffoonish prankster, a presence to be feared but also laughed at.

The first thing you notice when you see the Cadillacs live is the extent to which its lineup resembles that of a traditional salsa orchestra. There's the three-piece percussion section—congas, timbales, and trap drums—and the three-piece brass—sax, trumpet, and trombone. A tropically flavored orchestra placed at the service of rock 'n' roll.

Vicentico's proverbial rudeness comes effortlessly to him while he's performing. If a fan bothers him, he showers him with a cascade of crass Argentine epithets. At times, he may even threaten to punch him. But later that day, something changes. Vicentico sits down to talk to me, and suddenly he's a different person. We talk about music—better yet, we talk about the music that he likes. His expression softens. He speaks wistfully about the sounds that he grew up with, about his musical dreams. He tells me of the time the band began touring outside of Argentina and fell under the spell of the Afro-Caribbean groups they would see all over Latin America. The late Puerto Rican salsa singer Héctor Lavoé became an obligatory reference. The Cadillacs vowed to embrace the discipline of a barrio salsa combo, mastering their instruments to the sound of the clave.

But they were musically omnivorous, and the years of touring and recording allowed them to keep piling up the influences. Besides their time-tested love for ska, punk, reggae, and hard rock, they found the openness of mind to discover and assimilate genres as disparate as bossa nova, jazz, Mexican *rancheras*, cumbia, and the bitter tango of their native Buenos Aires. Their fusion became the epitome of *rock en español*—the reinterpretation of traditional rock formats through the prism of rootsy Latin genres.

I smile thinking of the unsuspecting BMG, which lured the Cadillacs away from Sony with an expensive multi-album deal. Clearly, they hoped that the band would release a number of "Matador" sound-alikes and continue to move in the easy-to-hum, ready-to-party vibe of the band's tropically flavored rock.

Instead, they got *Fabulosos calavera*.

✣

To this day, *Fabulosos calavera* is criticized by many Latin rock insiders as a vacuous album that strives to be clever and artistic by incorporating too many styles without a defined aesthetic direction.

Indeed, *Calavera* is not an accessible record. It demands time and patience. It's jarring and noisy, occasionally maddening, and drunk on its own sense of limitless discovery. It is a seminal *rock en español* record precisely because, in a sense, it is not even a rock record, but rather an aural snapshot of what contemporary Latin music is—or should be—all about.

Just like *Sgt. Pepper's*, *Calavera* is a conceptual album of sorts, not only because it is defined by a recurring theme (Death as the Eternal Jester), but because it delivers an aural journey with a distinct beginning, middle, and end.

Calavera is profoundly Argentinian in its sense of humor and cryptic local references, but at the same time it is a universal statement, paying tribute to a variety of pan-global sources, from the hardcore textures of "El carnicero de Giles" (The Butcher of Giles) to the *mariachi* strains of "Amnesia."

On "Niño diamante" (Diamond Boy), Vicentico lifts the shimmering piano pattern from Dave Brubeck's "Take Five" and runs with it, creating a crunchy slice of pop rock. The spirit of soundtrack composer Ennio Morricone haunts "Howen," an instrumental that could very well be the main theme for an imaginary spaghetti Western. Panamanian salsa singer Ruben Blades guests on the earthy "Hoy lloré canción" (Today I Wept a Song), giving full expression to the band's Afro-Caribbean leanings. An inevitable influence on Cianciarulo, visionary tango composer Astor Piazzolla is honored on the chaotic "Piazzolla," which samples the beginning of the maestro's *Tango: Zero Hour*. And the spirit of vintage tango informs the album's closing track, a delicate, melancholy ballad entitled "A.D.R.B."

All these references and outside influences are assimilated into the Cadillacs' cosmovision through the impossibly sad vocals of Vicentico, the lacerating guitar of brand-new member Ariel Minimal, and the production work of longtime collaborator K. C. Porter. *Calavera* is a raw, unconventional treasure from start to finish—miles away from the Cadillacs' calamitous beginnings fifteen years ago.

Vicentico and Cianciarulo were born two days apart in a Buenos Aires hospital. Like many an Argentine band, the Cadillacs began as a *barrio* group, a bunch of friends who were dreaming up band names long before they learned how to play their instruments.

In the beginning, the band was obsessed with ska and imitated their idols shamelessly. Their early gigs were reportedly dismal affairs, and many Argentine music fans began to laugh openly at these guys who would perform dressed in black, aping the ska revival of British bands like the Specials and Madness.

Released in 1986, the first Fabulosos Cadillacs album was entitled *Bares y fondas* (Bars and Saloons), a reference to the colorful neighborhoods where the band would get together and write songs such as "Mi novia se cayó en un pozo ciego" (My Girlfriend Fell in a Septic Tank) and "Yo no me sentaría en tu mesa" (I Wouldn't Sit on Your Table).

Today, *Bares y fondas* sounds primitive at best. But the album closes on a haunting note with "Basta de llamarme así"

(Stop Calling Me Like This), a song that offered a glimpse into Vicentico's remarkable imagination. The singer had lost his sister Tamara to a drug overdose. "Basta de llamarme así" was written as a reaction to her death:

Basta, basta de llamarme así
Mientras, te canto esta canción
En tu voz, en tu honor, o en la voz
De los que estén durmiendo allí

Stop, stop calling me like this
For now, I sing this song to you
In your voice, in your honor, or in the voice
Of those who sleep there

Throughout the eighties, the Cadillacs continued releasing albums, touring the provinces of Argentina, and eventually making a name for themselves across Latin America. They saw music as a serious profession, and worked hard to become better composers and instrumentalists. The Cadillacs' artistic success, in other words, was not the result of spontaneous genius, but rather the fruit of perseverance—an effort of such titanic proportions, in fact, that it arguably caused the band to break up when it finally made it big.

By the time the Cadillacs released *El león* (The Lion) in 1992, they were ready to make a major statement. Something had clicked. The key to inspiration was not ska anymore, but rather the rich tapestry of Latin America, both in terms of its music (salsa, samba, Astor Piazzolla, Ruben Blades) and its thinkers (the poetic work of journalist Eduardo Galeano was admittedly a huge influence on Cianciarulo). *El león* did indeed signify the birth of Latin rock as a mature genre. *Rock en español* was not about imitating the Cure or the Rolling Stones any more. The Latin beat was cool to this new generation of rockers, and they expressed their feelings of discovery with pride and an exuberant, party-like atmosphere.

To this day, many Latin rock connoisseurs (the same ones who decry *Fabulosos calavera* as a total mess) think of *El león* as one of the key works in the genre, and the Cadillacs' finest hour. I tend to disagree, if only because *El león* was the promise of so much more to come.

Commercially speaking, the Cadillacs' best moment was the single "Matador," which became a pop anthem of massive proportions in Latin America and Spain. It opened a lot of doors for the band, and allowed them to find the courage to experiment even further with unusual sounds and textures. A few critics complained that "Matador" shamelessly ripped off the songs of lesser-known Brazilian *batucada* ensemble Olodum. Indeed, there's a striking similarity between the track's propulsive beat and Olodum's material. But "Matador" was much more than just a cool *batucada*-based pop song, since it included the unforgettable vocals of Vicentico (part Rubén Blades, part tango crooner) and his politically charged toasting.

Expanding on the carnivalesque atmosphere of "Matador," 1995's extravagant *Rey azúcar* (King Sugar) was the band's last step before achieving the maturity of *Calavera*. Overproduced by former Talking Heads members Chris Frantz and Tina Weymouth, the album included cameos by the Clash's Mick Jones on the salsa-tinged "Mal bicho"

(Mean Bug) and Blondie's Deborah Harry on a headache-inducing version of the Beatles' "Strawberry Fields Forever."

The tour to promote *Fabulosos calavera* was a triumph. During a show at the six-thousand-seat Universal Amphitheatre in Los Angeles, Vicentico was in rare form, showering the audience with his usual deadpan nonsensical comments, but still serious enough to offer shattering performances of the electrifying "Saco azul" (Blue Coat) and the lilting "Estrella de mar" (Sea Star), both from *Rey azúcar*. When performing the *Calavera* tunes, he would contort his body as if pierced by a beam of deadly light. The tragic spirit of tango was a constant presence in the show, not only through Vicentico's vocal delivery, but also when Cianciarulo performed a riveting version of "Piazzolla."

The concert's best moments betrayed the influence of hardcore. Just like in much of post-punk pop, chunks of blinding beauty could be found in the relentless sonic mayhem.

Vicentico did not seem to enjoy touring. I interviewed him again during the *Calavera* tour and he appeared tired. We sat outside a Hollywood hotel where the band was staying. He smoked a couple of cigarettes and looked down at the ground with his usual meditative expression. "It's some sort of constant purgatory," he told me. "To tell you the truth, there's a lot of hotels all over America that are quite sinister. All you see is a bunch of lifeless, obese people sitting by the pool waiting for something to happen.

"We still try to have a good time while on tour. We assembled a little band on the tour bus, just a simple setup—piano, bass, percussion. We play music. We watch movies and shoot home videos."

Still, he sounded very upbeat about the new songs that the band had been recording in Buenos Aires. "As a band, we're getting further and further away from rock 'n' roll. We had this ridiculous idea of having a farm as the backdrop for the tunes. A farm complete with animals that play musical instruments. It's really silly, as you can see, very nonsensical. That's why the new songs are loaded with samples of birds and animal calls. A bizarre invention, isn't it?"

I asked him about BMG, which was looking for a "Matador"-sized single to recoup its investment.

"They certainly expect us to deliver an album that sounds like the commercial, easy-to-sell Cadillacs," he admitted. "But the thing is, this new music I'm telling you about is even more difficult than *Calavera*, so I don't know how it will all work out. Our new music belongs to no genre. We could always do a commercial record if we wanted to. I still have the hope that we'll do the record that we want to make and that it will sell well. It was the same with *Fabulosos calavera*. Everybody started saying that it was a weird record, and yet it won a Grammy and sold a pretty good number of copies."

But something happened on the way to the studio. In 1999, the Cadillacs released *La marcha del golazo solitario* (The March of the Lonely Goal), the most exquisite follow-up one could have hoped for. To this day, it remains the group's studio swan song.

If *Calavera* displayed the bravado of a rock 'n' roll group that has achieved total control over its instrumental capabilities, *La marcha* showcased a total indifference to the fans. It is the least self-conscious chapter in the Cadillacs' book.

Unlike *Calavera*, which left no stone unturned in the process of scavenging musical genres, *La marcha* stays rooted in only one major influence: the school of sentimental pop that flourished in the late sixties and early seventies, taking lounge music to a supreme level of emotionality. The album's sweeping "C.J." sounds uncannily similar to any of the greatest hits by Brazilian crooner Roberto Carlos. And the jazz funk of "Cebolla" (Onion) echoes the early (and best) albums by Mexican singer José José.

Lyrically, the record is supported by the contrasting styles of Vicentico and Cianciarulo. Capello's compositions are dark and abstract. Cianciarulo, on the other hand, is in a decidedly optimistic mood. His opening "La vida" (Life) is the kind of bittersweet meditation on life you would expect from a vintage *bossa nova* tune, something straight out of *Black Orpheus*. "Oh, life/We all want to touch the sky," Cianciarulo tells us before giving positive feedback on the unwritten laws of fate and karma.

Similarly, "Vos sabés" (You Know) is a simple, poetic melody conveying the indescribable feelings of fulfillment that come with parenthood:

> *El amor de un padre a un hijo*
> *No se puede comparar*
> *Es mucho más que todo*
> *No, si vos sabés*

> *The love of a father for his child*
> *Cannot be compared*

It's bigger than anything
I'll never feel lonely again

Elsewhere *La marcha* still betrays the afterthoughts of the *Calavera* experience. "El baile del mar" (The Dance of the Sea) could easily be an outtake from those sessions, and "La rosca" (The Screw) continues the band's obsession with tango. But the closing instrumental "Alamo" is the most sentimental piece of music the group ever recorded.

La marcha del golazo solitario was a critical success and sold moderately well. But the band failed once again to connect with a mainstream audience outside of Argentina. The artistic achievement of the last two albums had empowered them to continue to ignore their fans' expectations, follow their heart, and make the music that they really enjoyed making. Now it was time for them to strike out on their own.

There was a problem, though: as part of its contract with BMG, the band still owed the label two albums.

The band found a Machiavellian solution. They celebrated their fifteenth anniversary with a massive show in Buenos Aires, recorded the gig in its entirety, and released it in 2000 as two separate albums, wryly titled *Hola* (Hello) and *Chau* (Goodbye).

The most interesting thing about these records is how the band's old hits and the vastly superior new tunes function as a cohesive whole when accompanied by the thunderous noise of thousands of euphoric Argentinians.

Chau begins gloriously with a soaring "Manuel Santillán, el león" chanted word for word by the fans. "Estoy harto de verte con otros" (I'm Sick and Tired of Seeing You with Others) off 1987's *Yo te avisé* (I Told You So) is followed by the noise of "Piraña, todos los Argentinos somos D.T." (Piranha,

All Argentines Are Soccer Coaches)—an example of *La marcha del golazo solitario* at its most disjointed.

Toward the end of the show, when Capello has already performed the crowd favorites "Carnaval toda la vida" (Carnival Forever) and "Matador," he delivers a memorable farewell message, condemning Argentina's never-ending political corruption. "What we have here is the real world," Capello says while the band performs the last bars of the moody "Los condenaditos" (The Little Condemned Ones). "It's not the world of the fucking senators and politicians. This is the world where we should live. The world of music and art. Our world."

It's a heart-wrenching moment, proving that the Cadillacs hadn't lost an ounce of idealism since their inception fifteen years ago. Like the best of *rock en español*, their music made you dance and ponder weighty issues at the same time.

What could the Cadillacs do next?

Free of the restraints of a record label contract, they talked of forming their own label for the release of their next album.

In the meantime, they embarked on an endless tour to promote the live albums, making good money off the well-attended gigs—but leaving their set list virtually unchanged for a couple of years. Unintentionally, they began sounding like a nostalgia act, basking in past glories. Yet the shows remained blistering and idiosyncratic, showcasing the band's total disregard for the conventions of rock 'n' roll. More than ever before, the band's capricious changes in pace and style, its occasional irruption into *nuevo tango* territory, the mocking military marches (complete with the pseudo solemnity of a polished brass section), and Vicentico's erratic bits of spoken poetry provided the perfect aural representation of the chaos and subversion of daily life in Latin America.

The Cadillacs negotiated recording an album with visionary *rock en español* producer Gustavo Santaolalla, who had already produced a number of tracks from *El león*. But Santaolalla was busy with a number of other projects, including Café Tacvba (see next chapter). At the same time, the Cadillacs thought that they were ready to produce their new music themselves.

The tour finally came to an end. Cianciarulo, tired of Argentina's socioeconomic crisis, decided to move his family to Mexico for a short while—they stayed in his wife's native Monterrey. Vicentico delved into movie acting, and then began recording his first solo album. Soon, a message on the band's Web site delivered, more than anything else, the implicit message that things were everything but OK:

"Fabulosos Cadillacs have not broken up."

At least not officially. In fact, the band had simply ceased to exist; its members embarked on an agreed hiatus with no expiration date.

The year was 2001. To me, the Cadillacs represented the very future of Latin rock. I spoke with both Cianciarulo and Vicentico and got their version of what was essentially the band's breakup.

"Sometimes life puts you in a standby sort of mood," was the first thing that Cianciarulo told me over the phone from Monterrey. "And I guess we're all responding to a moment in our lives where we're meant to develop stuff on our own. It wasn't planned that way. It just happened."

"It was just too many years of playing together," added Vicentico on a placid Buenos Aires morning during a conversation that was interrupted when he had to pick up his son from school. "The group's success gave us financial security—but it ended up being like a house that's too comfortable for your own good. I think it's healthy for all of us to get out of the house and see what's happening out there."

Eager to explore his love of jazz, tango, and South American folklore, Cianciarulo released a solo album, *El marplatense* (The Man from Mar Del Plata), joined by a trio he named Flavio Calaveralma, a juxtaposition of the words *calavera* (skull) and *alma* (soul). Since then, he has released another album, 2004's *Cachivache!* (Junk!).

Soon, Vicentico also had a self-titled solo album of his own. Whereas *El marplatense* had the feel of a cult record, *Vicentico* boasted the kind of pop sensibility and slick production values that would ease the singer into a highly successful career as a solo artist.

"I trust the Cadillacs will make another album in a couple of years," Vicentico told me then. "On the other hand, I can't imagine not recording more solo albums. From the beginning it's been pretty obvious to me that this record is the first of many. I have other, more complex songs that I'd like to do on my own."

Stylistically, *Vicentico* was light years away from the Cadillacs' eclecticism. Still, the record functioned as a luscious consolation prize for all the fans who had been eagerly anticipating a new Cadillacs release. Anchored on his unmistakable, sadder-than-sad vocals, the collection offers a cleaner, back-to-basics version of the group's trademark sound. The emphasis is on percolating, percussion-friendly rhythms such as the murga and the samba, as well as the Cadillacs' connection with Argentinian tango through its obsessive reliance on nostalgia as the most desirable of emotional states. Much of the album works its charm in unassuming ways, from the lilting love lament "La única culpable" (The Only Guilty One) to "Se despierta la ciudad" (The City Wakes Up), a furious mambo with lightning-fast piano and lyrics that cleverly address Argentina's current sociopolitical crisis.

Vicentico suggests a sincere tribute to seventies Latin lounge pop, when sensitive crooners such as Nino Bravo wooed South American housewives with a warm, classy, and melodious sound. "There's a lot of Roberto Carlos in this album," Capello said during our conversation. "I just love that seventies stuff, the way it allows you, emotionally speaking, to move back and forth between your childhood and your adult years."

And would the old Vicentico, the sarcastic youngster who sang "Mi novia se cayó en un pozo ciego," approve of such an openly sentimental album? "I think he would have liked it," he laughed.

Vicentico's first test as a solo performer came when he presented the album live with his new band at a Buenos Aires theatre. The packed crowd included the Argentine media and a bunch of fellow musicians. "All of a sudden, I looked at the audience and saw a few of my bandmates watching the show," he recalled. "And I couldn't help thinking that it was a weird, totally distorted situation, almost out of a bad dream. But things are what they are. If part of this whole experience involves my friends coming to see me with a 'What-am-I-doing-here' expression on their face, then so be it. Music, when it's done with love, always ends up saving the day in the end."

Vicentico's Los Angeles debut as a solo performer was certainly inauspicious. In 2002, he performed in front of six thousand people with the Cadillacs. A year later, he brought his new band to Hollywood's Knitting Factory. The club's intimate floor was half empty.

Accompanied by nine superlative instrumentalists—including a dizzying five-piece percussion section fronted by drummer Daniel Buira—Vicentico offered soulful renditions of the new tunes, including a wistful "Vamos" (Let's Go), complete with plaintive touches of flügelhorn.

When it came time to satisfy hardcore Cadillacs fans, he took a creative approach, delivering pared-down versions of the oldies, such as "Padre nuestro" (Our Father) and "Basta de llamarme así," as well as a particularly paranoid reading of "Saco azul." Strangely enough, it was the new tunes that stood out, commanding attention through their sophisticated arrangements and emotional immediacy. Vicentico was on his way to a highly successful solo career.

Los rayos (The Rays), which included a Rubén Blades cover ("Tiburón" [Shark], from the salsero's peak years with the Fania label), was released in 2004. This album continued favoring a more mainstream sound, one that could appeal to the old Cadillacs fan base as well as new listeners from all possible age brackets. The Cadillacs were history. Vicentico has become a true Latin American pop star.

And *rock en español* may never be the same.

Café Tacvba

I NEVER THOUGHT I could like an album so much.

It's a rainy evening in Van Nuys, California. The year is 1999. I've been invited to the recording studio where Mexican quartet Café Tacvba is putting the finishing touches on its new, highly ambitious double album.

As a rock journalist, you get invited to preview albums in the studio quite often. Publicists and musicians understand that music sounds much better when it's freshly made, blaring from the expensive speakers of a quality studio. The artist is usually head over heels in love with his brand new creation. The future, at that moment, appears limitless and endlessly pleasurable. You have to be a tough-skinned cynic not to be swept away by the sheer euphoria of the moment.

I'm keeping all that in mind while trying to behave like the seasoned, heard-it-all-before professional that I'm supposed to be. But I can't. I am genuinely stunned. This music is heavenly.

I'm sitting in front of the soundboard. The band is taking a break. Longtime Tacvba producer Gustavo Santaolalla has just played a few tracks for me. He looks at my bewildered expression and smiles, very much aware that he is making *rock en español* history.

Revés/Yosoy (Backwards/I Am) is two contrasting discs, the yin and yang of Tacvba's own version of the Beatles' *White Album*. (Yes—if the Cadillacs' *Fabulosos calavera* is *rock en español*'s version of *Sgt. Pepper's*, it would appear that the genre's *Abbey Road* has yet to be recorded.) *Revés* is a CD of dissonant instrumentals. Mesmerizing as it is, you will probably listen to the whole thing once or twice in your life. Why? Because *Revés* is actually nothing but an introduction to the treasures on the second disc. The solemn strings of guest artist Kronos Quartet, the lightness of a clarinet ensemble, and the brash cacophony of most of the tracks seem to serve a definite purpose: to rid your ears of any prejudice, preparing you for the meatier side of the program.

Even by Tacvba's standards, the fifteen songs that make up *Yosoy* are surprisingly rich. Unlike most *rock en español*, these compositions achieve a perfect marriage between melodic exploration and expressive lyrics.

Santaolalla plays the opening track for me, "El padre" (The Father). The format is pure Mexican folk—a traditional *huapango*. But this one comes with drum machines and eerie guitar effects. It tells the story of a man who one day wakes up to see that his face in the mirror bears an uncanny resemblance to his father's. His voice sounds just like his father's too. He has become the one person he hated the most. There's no way back. Tacvba has grown up, and observes its unavoidable maturity with amusement.

"La locomotora" (The Locomotive), the track that ended up being the collection's sole hit single, was written by keyboardist Emmanuel Del Real—Tacvba's bona fide hitmaker. In typical Tacvba fashion, it features a trashy drum loop instead of live drums. The absence of a drummer was the band's identifiable quirk from its inception in the late eighties to the violent switch in musical direction that shook Tacvba up somewhere around 2002.

The wonderfully quirky "El hombre impasible" with its sweetly psychedelic chorus ("I am the impossible/impassible man") has 1968-era Beatles written all over it, while "La muerte chiquita" (The Little Death) is an elegant waltz mirroring Latin America's morbid preoccupation with the relationship between sex and death. As close to hummable pop as the disc ever gets, "Dos niños" (Two Children) explores the sexual awakening of two teenagers with disturbingly upbeat instrumentation. Although Tacvba came of age in the aftermath of punk and electronica, its vivifying connection to Latin American folklore keeps reappearing when you least expect it to, as on the lyrical "El río" (The River).

Nothing is what it appears to be in Tacvba's labyrinth of sounds. The set is marked by all sorts of eccentric creative decisions. The last three songs of *Yosoy*, for instance, are divided into thirty-nine separate tracks, so that the total can reach the mystical number fifty-two, representing the cycles of the Aztec calendar.

Six years after I sat speechless in that recording studio, *Revés/Yosoy* continues to inspire me, its vision unmatched by anything that Latin rock has given us since then. The collection has a life of its own, and continues to change with the times. Yes, it was a commercial disappointment at the center of yet another failed attempt to engineer a *faux* crossover of Latin rock to the American mainstream. Who cares? An exhilarating masterpiece, it is probably the pinnacle of the entire movement.

Earlier during that rainy evening in Van Nuys, I sat with half of Tacvba and watched them eat tacos in the studio's kitchen, exchanging stories about the most hilarious (and unabashedly morbid) *corridos* that they had heard in recent times. Emmanuel Del Real and bass player Quique Rangel treated me with friendly respect, turning what could have been a formal interview into a casual chat. Singer Rubén Albarrán and guitarist (and Quique's brother) Joselo Rangel were in Mexico City working on another project. Meme (as Del Real is affectionately called) and Quique had stayed behind, finishing up the album with Santaolalla and his creative partner Aníbal Kerpel. Half an hour later, the three of us stepped inside the mixing room. Santaolalla and Kerpel had locked horns during the mixing of a forty-second-long tune. Entitled "Esperando" (Waiting), the intimate song was a solo effort by Quique, who had performed a timid vocal debut accompanying himself on the upright bass.

Santaolalla had decided to create a theatrical sound effect by pushing the bass to the forefront of the mix. And Kerpel was quick in voicing his disagreement. "It's too loud," he said. "The bass would never sound like that in real life."

"That's precisely the point," Santaolalla answered laconically. "Roll the tape," he ordered the tape operator with a sudden change of tone that nobody would have dared to contradict.

The track was mastered, and as soon as the operator played it back, it was quite obvious that Santaolalla had been right. His risky decision enriched the tune with an airy feeling, as if Quique had recorded the song within the blurry boundaries of a dream.

The release of *Revés/Yosoy* on Warner Bros. Records was the result of a bidding war that saw companies such as Virgin and Universal Music Group fighting for Tacvba. At the time, Warner thought that it had a major alternative radio hit in its hands, something like the Mexican answer to Stereolab. But the band members were understandably skeptical. "We'll see how much effort they put into promoting it," Albarrán told me at the time.

Onstage, the singer is a certified eccentric, performing in bizarre hats, colorful clothes, or even a rooster mask. He also has the habit of changing names from project to project. He has been known as Cosme, Anómimo, Gallo Gass (Rooster Gas—therefore the rooster mask), Rita Cantalagua, Elfego Buendía, and a variety of other monikers. But on the phone, through years of extensive interviews, he has always been extremely sweet, even shy. "They are real gentlemen," Kerpel will tell me every time I comment on the humbleness that has defined all four Tacubos throughout our meetings.

"The people at Warner are enthusiastic about it," Albarrán emphasized. "But seeing is believing."

Tacvba had nothing to fear, though. Its pedigree and reputation transcended any label's commercial expectations. "They never sold millions of records, but they are still considered one of the real heavyweights of *rock en español*," Kerpel reminded me. "They don't need to have a number-one album in order to be a number-one band."

"I have the feeling that today's listeners are more than prepared for a record like ours," Albarrán told me with exaggerated optimism. "In fact, I still think we could have gone a step further with our experiments. Everything has already been done in music anyway. You just come up with a different way of doing things."

Café Tacuba's (the original spelling was with a "u" instead of a "v") self-titled debut came out in 1992. Although it included the hit single "La chica banda" (*Banda* Girl) and did a great job at introducing the quartet's twisted sense of humor to the world, it felt somewhat hesitant and unrealized.

Then came *Ré*.

Released in 1994, two years after Fabulosos Cadillacs' *El león*, *Ré* was a key album for the genre, a winning mixture of retro Latin styles and palatable Anglo idioms. Naming specific genres is somewhat preposterous when describing this album—Tacvba covered them all in a whimsical, twenty-song cycle that included gems such as the reckless "La ingrata" (Ungrateful), the *banda sinaloense* meets ska noise of "El fin de la infancia" (Childhood's End), and the utterly endearing melodica line of "Las flores" (The Flowers). Listening to the whole thing in one sitting, it was easy to realize that Tacvba had humble aspirations: they just wanted to change the world.

In fact, many consider *Ré* to be the apex of the genre. I am partial to its follow-up, the less grandiose *Avalancha de éxitos* (Avalanche of Hits).

Released in 1996, *Avalancha* was a collection of cover songs that the foursome recorded when they found themselves stuck working on their original material. Five of its eight songs became hit singles: the eccentric "Chilanga banda" (Mexico City Band), the furious "No controles" (Don't Control), the darkly humorous classic by eighties Mexican group Botellita de Jerez "Alármala de tos," the earthy Juan Luis Guerra composition "Ojalá que llueva café" (I Wish It Would Rain Coffee), and a tender version of "Cómo te extraño mi amor" (How I Miss You My Love) by venerable Argentine popster Leo Dan.

Avalancha went platinum in Mexico, and it cemented the band's presence in the Latin rock landscape. Soon enough, rave reviews appeared in mainstream Anglo publications such as *Rolling Stone* and *Spin*. It was becoming clear that you didn't need to understand the lyrics in order to appreciate Tacvba's hip sensibility.

The band's success and a grueling tour that took a whole year to finish brought inevitable tension among its members. For a while, it wasn't clear if Tacvba would remain together.

Then, the recording of the instrumental tracks that make up *Revés* revivified the group.

"It was like starting on a blank page again," Albarrán told me. "Recording *Revés* had a medicinal sort of effect, because it relieved us of the friction and the bad feelings that were rooted within the group. It made us remember the reasons why we like each other, why we clicked together in the first place."

At that point, it was decided that the album would be a double set. For the second disc, the quartet recorded the songs that had been abandoned in 1995 in favor of the *Avalancha* album. "Once we felt cured by the experience of *Revés*, we returned to those songs with renewed strength," said Albarrán.

When it came time to tour behind *Revés/Yosoy*, the band debated on how to present the new material without alienating the longtime fans. "We have absolutely no idea on how to go about it," Albarrán admitted. "Making this album has been an arduous process. Now we have to sit down and plot the course of our live shows."

I saw the band live at the Sun Theatre, a huge venue in Anaheim. The concert challenged listeners as much as it rewarded them. Alternating melodramatic intensity with a remarkable levity of spirit and *avant-garde* minimalism with a populist attitude, Tacvba showcased its maturity. Never a band to betray its fans' deepest desires, the quartet offered a healthy selection of the old favorites, including the majority of *Avalancha de éxitos*. But the show's most intense moments came when the quartet responded with ballsy assuredness to the challenge of reproducing the kaleidoscopic textures of the new album in a concert setting. Live, the instrumentals sounded like the fever-induced nightmares of a college student who has spent a whole day listening to Kraftwerk, Robert Fripp, and Stockhausen. The audience gave an unusually positive response to a twenty-minute passage of electronic distortion and drum machine rage that seemed to belong at a drum+bass club instead of a rock 'n' roll concert. The songs from *Yosoy*, on the other hand, offered exquisite melodies within a more conventional context. The capacity audience applauded the quartet's every move, and the show itself mirrored the wave of creativity that Tacvba was enjoying at the time. Unfortunately, the album's lackluster sales would send the group in search of a more commercial sound.

Quieren rock, putos?

Wearing that ridiculous rooster mask, Albarrán (or should we say Gallo Gass) taunted the audience at the Hollywood Palladium in 2003, where the quartet had just finished performing a slow number in front of thousands of noisy fans who were clearly interested in more raucous material.

Want rock, fuckers?

Yes, they wanted rock. And rock they did, the four Tacubos. More conventionally, in fact, than ever before. After spending over a decade developing a loopy, deliciously oblique sound cemented on the bouncy charms of a drum machine, the foursome had decided to turn the tables on us and bring a live drummer in.

Onstage at the Palladium, Tacvba became a quintet, and the drummer's relentless 4/4 attack limited the scope and the airiness of the band's music. A song like "La locomotora"—frantic and eccentric in its original incarnation—sounded strangely flat. A medley of venerable *rock en español* classics that included snippets from the Cadillacs' "Matador" and Aterciopelados' "Bolero falaz" was equally uninspired, almost pedestrian.

There was no doubt about it. Tacvba had taken its first, calamitous artistic misstep.

The first disappointment arrived in the guise of *Vale callampa* (It's Worthless), a bewildering 2002 EP with four songs paying tribute to Chilean group Los Tres. Even the foursome's knack for quirky arrangements couldn't disguise the capricious nature of the project and the questionable quality of the original material.

Three years later, *Cuatro caminos* (Four Roads) offered a perverse antidote to the lofty heights of the past. Here was a novel concept: a no-frills, run-of-the-mill rock record. Tacvba with drums, minus the Mexican influences.

"We have reinvented ourselves," Alabarrán told me when I explained to him my doubts about the new record. "And that makes us happy. We were able to free ourselves from the traps in which we usually fall. Regardless of its commercial potential this one's been a successful project."

"I find it surprising that after fourteen years of playing together, we finally made the kind of record that we liked listening to when we were teenagers," added Del Real. "Back then, I listened to bands like Led Zeppelin, Iron Maiden, and Judas Priest."

The accessible nature of these songs opened up new roads for Tacvba. The first single, a jarring experiment in electronic exuberance named "Eo," got radio airplay on the strength of its cheesy, eighties-influenced keyboard sounds and Albarrán's Donald-Duck-on-acid vocalizing that praised the art of the *sonideros* or sound makers, Mexico's own answer to the DJ phenomenon.

The album's slower tunes showcase Tacvba at its tuneful best—it's quite easy to fall in love with the pastoral beauty of "Mediodía" (Noon), which uses the shimmering sound of bells to evoke the vibe of a peaceful afternoon in Mexico City. Its lyrics find Quique observing the view from the window of his house and wondering why he has no one to share it with.

And on the record's most painfully honest song, "Tomar el fresco" (Taking Some Air), guitarist Joselo refers to the one-year sabbatical that the band took just before returning to record *Cuatro caminos*:

> *Si no regreso no pasa nada*
> *Tarde o temprano*
> *Alguien me viene a suplantar*
> *Que no?*

> *If I fail to return, nothing will happen*
> *Sooner than later*
> *Someone else will replace me*
> *Isn't that so?*

"That's what I love about this record," exclaimed Del Real. "Not only did we make a straight-ahead rock album, but we also included personal confessions that go way beyond anything that we expressed in our lyrics before. It almost works as a confessionary of sorts."

"Feeling claustrophobic is natural when you've been in a band for so long," commented Albarrán. "Perhaps our biggest achievement has been staying together. It takes a lot of balls to make compromises and accept the others' decisions."

Is the simplicity of *Cuatro caminos* an inevitable reaction to the commercial failure of the *Revés/Yosoy* experience?

"We always assume that people will understand our records," said Albarrán. "But we're often wrong. And we were definitely wrong this time. We weren't able to find the appropriate channels for people to connect with the record. We failed to realize that maybe our fans weren't interested in a CD of instrumental pieces."

"The disappointment didn't last long," Albarrán continued. "Internally, as a band, we considered *Revés/Yosoy* a success, because making it was like medicine to us. It had a healing effect on the way in which we related to music, the way in which we interacted as composers. That record was good for us."

"The record company didn't quite know what to do with it," Del Real told me. "Sure enough, it was a complicated record, somewhat inaccessible. But it also gained us a lot of respect and appreciation. We spent two years touring behind it. Now people know that we're capable of many different things. After *Cuatro caminos*, we could very well do a record that's all acoustic, or maybe one that draws solely from folk-lore. Who knows? Even I couldn't tell you what lies ahead in Tacvba's future."

And the drums?

Ah, those drums. It was Albarrán's idea to bring them in, by the way. And he doesn't regret it.

"Think of a painter who has a very special relationship with a specific color—say, orange," he explained when questioned about the decision to change Tacvba's sound. "For a moment in his career, he abandons orange altogether and begins using other colors . . . blues and greens. When he returns to orange, he will have renewed his relationship to that color.

"In our case, I felt that it was time to give the sequencers and drum machines a rest. Playing with a live drummer was an amazing discovery for us. There's a number of things that you lose, but I think it's perfect for us right now. The day we return to the drum machines, we will have a completely new perspective on things."

"At first I felt like I was losing a limb," said Del Real, who was always in charge of programming and triggering the sequencers in concert. "With the drummer, we all play louder now. It's a different experience, but eventually you get used to it and fall in love with the new sonics. I still miss the drum machine, though."

"Some songs work better than others," Albarrán concluded. "But I'll gladly exchange that for the enjoyment that we're experiencing. Maybe we're losing something on the artistic side, but that's OK. What we originally tried to say with the drum machines has been preserved. It's inside a hard drive or a memory card. We can return to it whenever we please. Maybe that's why we are not experiencing the change like a loss, but rather like a breath of fresh air."

❧

In 2004, the four Tacubos realized that the band's fifteenth anniversary loomed on the horizon. As a result, they decided to organize an intimate celebration—a party, perhaps, where they could perform for a select group of family and friends.

But the low-key party turned into something much bigger when Tacvba was booked for two sold-out shows at the huge Palacio de los Deportes—the de rigueur rock venue in Mexico City.

"Two months before the actual show we contemplated the possibility of filming and recording the whole thing, regardless of any live album that could result from it," Del Real told me over the phone during a conversation we shared in 2005. "We decided to bankroll the project ourselves, then take it to the record company and see if they liked what they saw."

The resulting shows lasted four hours each. A number of famous Mexican rockers (Roco from Maldita Vecindad, Alejandro Lora from El Tri) were on hand to pay their respects and sing with Tacvba onstage.

In the end, Universal Music executives loved the finished project so much that they decided to release it in three different versions—all of them titled *Un viaje* (A Journey).

Consumers could choose between the two-CD live album with twenty-nine tracks; the DVD with twenty-three of those tracks and a number of features such as extensive interviews and a visit to Tacvba's studio; and a box set that included the previous three discs plus an extra CD with seven bonus tracks culled from the same shows.

Del Real, who lists Rush's *Exit Stage Left* and the Beatles' *Live at the Hollywood Bowl* as his two favorite live albums, is no stranger to the devotion that concert recordings can ignite in a fan. In 2002, he took a leave of absence from the recording of *Cuatro caminos* in order to fly to Mexico and see Rush live for the first time in his life.

"As a kid, I had actual dreams about seeing Rush in concert and hanging out backstage with Neil Peart," he explained. "The experience of seeing them in concert was exactly the way I had imagined it. I felt like a teenager again. Recording our own live album was a way of sharing with the fans a moment that was extremely emotional for us."

Commercially, *Un viaje* was extremely successful. In artistic terms, it is something of a disappointment.

The DVD portion of the concert suffers from shoddy production values. Watching Tacvba perform on their home turf, surrounded by an impressive list of guest stars and thousands of adoring fans is bound to be an emotional experience. But the DVD's sound is poor and the images on this multi-camera production are occasionally grainy and clumsily put together.

Sonically, the CDs are noticeably better. But previous Tacvba shows have boasted state-of-the-art quality. Recording such an expansive live collection at a less-than-favorable venue may have been a mistake.

"It was the worst place that I've ever been for a live recording," Tony Peluso, the band's longtime sound engineer, told me. "That place is not meant for music. It's built like an echo chamber and has a seven-second delay. But that's what Rubén wanted to capture: a moment in time."

According to Peluso, the initial part of the first evening wasn't even recorded. The engineer's team was still getting used to the fifty mike lines and the sixty thousand screaming fans. But Peluso is quick to point out that *Un viaje* is, for the most part, a real live recording. Most so-called concert albums by mainstream pop acts are tinkered with in post-production.

"Ninety percent of what we recorded during those two nights is there," he explains. "We replaced a couple of acoustic guitars and a few vocal lines. I told the band that we could make it sound better, but they insisted that this was all about the energy of the performance coming through. If there was a mistake, they didn't want to polish it."

As a testament of the Tacvba live experience, *Un viaje* emphasizes the eccentric nature of the band.

There's Albarrán's peculiar choice of wardrobe (he appears wearing a skirt during part of the show). A zany version of Los Tres' "Déjate caer" (Let Yourself Fall) ends with the band triggering a prerecorded disco loop, walking to the front of the stage, and engaging in a robotic, coordinated little dance. And there's the singer's nonsensical—and seemingly endless—stage banter, filled with silly free associations and a poignant message to the fans ("we used to think that we'd end up performing solely at friends' parties").

You would think that the fact that the band has managed to survive—let alone become one of its genre's commercial heavyweights—is nothing less than a miracle.

"All of us grew up listening to infectious music," said Del Real, expressing his disagreement in a subtle way. "From the Stones and Devo to José José, Los Tigres del Norte, and Antonio Carlos Jobim. Think about it: all those artists are accessible and have sold a lot of records. It's true—we never thought that we would end up connecting with radio and television. But the moment you realize that people like what you do, you become conscious of the fact that you want to be both artistic and commercial at the same time. We have never been into rejecting our own audience."

The Palacio de los Deportes gigs had a positive effect on the band. During the subsequent tour in 2005 to promote *Un viaje*, the Tacubos were in high spirits, enjoying the opportunity to celebrate their own catalogue. Early songs such as "Noche oscura" (Dark Night), "Rarotonga," and "María" shone like never before. Better yet, the loud drums finally sounded right—the band had found a new balance as a quintet. Fans can expect a new album in 2006 by a group that continues to be Latin rock's most ambitious and visionary act.

Aterciopelados

RIGHT NOW ANDREA Echeverri should be experiencing a bad case of stage fright. She should look pale, maybe even sweat a little. She should be crossing herself and looking at her band members for moral support.

On a sunny afternoon, in the Burbank studios of the *Tonight Show*, the tall, lanky, bohemian-looking *chanteuse* from Colombia is waiting patiently for Jay Leno to introduce her band, *rock en español* favorite Aterciopelados, to mainstream America.

Jay Leno. The *Tonight Show*. This is the moment that the entire Latin rock movement has been waiting for and it's happening now, in 2001.

Somewhere in the backstage area, I meet with Julio Correal, the group's affable manager. He's pacing up and down. "I've never been so nervous in my entire life," he says. He notes that Aterciopelados has flown twelve hours from Colombia solely for an engagement that will end up lasting a grand total of three and a half minutes. "That's how much this means to us," he adds nervously.

At this moment, of course, it would be foolish to question the validity of this investment. Aterciopelados' appearance will mark the first time a Latin rock act has been booked on the *Tonight Show* (Mexico's Maná once appeared with Santana, but the group lacks Aterciopelados' street cred and pedigree within the movement). Coincidentally, the taping is taking place on the same day that the band's fifth album, *Gozo poderoso* (Powerful Delight), is being released in the United States. We're at the highest point of an aggressive, four-month promotional campaign that has seen two major labels (Arista and BMG Latin) as well as one of the most reputable publicity firms in the Latin music world joining forces to sell this idiosyncratic group to American audiences.

Echeverri should be having the first signs of a nervous breakdown. But she isn't. Her attitude, in fact, tells me that the invasion of North America is not, at the moment, high on her priority list.

I climb the stairs to her dressing room and I see her waving at me, wearing a gorgeous traditional garment from the Guajira region of Colombia. Calm and collected. Greeting me with the same warm smile and inner peace that she has shown in our repeated meetings over the last six years.

Instead of talking about the upcoming performance, she worries about getting enough of an herbal medicine that, she thinks, would really help her ailing father in Bogotá.

"At this point, we just want to sell enough records for things to function smoothly and to be able to keep making music," she will tell me the following day over lunch, sitting next to Aterciopelados' other half, bassist (and former boyfriend) Héctor Buitrago. "We don't want to be millionaires," she emphasizes. "We're very happy in Colombia. We love our houses and our significant others. It's nice to come here for a few gigs, but staying in Latin America is key to us. Playing somewhere like Costa Rica, for instance—there's a very special satisfaction that comes from something like that."

Wise words indeed. A few minutes later, Aterciopelados' performance at Leno's show would clearly indicate that the band—and the whole of Latin rock—is definitely not ready for mainstream success.

In the beginning, there was punk.

Echeverri and Buitrago were boyfriend and girlfriend in early nineties Bogotá. Their first group was named Delia y los Aminoácidos. The second one was going to be called Ater-

© María Madrigal/*La Banda Elastica*

ciopelada Flor de la Pasión (The Velvety Flower of Passion), a moniker that revealed the pair's mocking affection for all things kitsch. They finally stuck with Aterciopelados and released a rough debut album, *Con el corazón en la mano* (Heart in Hand), in 1994.

Much like its predecessor, 1995's *El Dorado* had a half finished air to it. But it included Aterciopelados' brilliant first hit, "Bolero falaz" (Deceitful Bolero). The duo had finally discovered its true niche: combining rock with a postmodern, highly ironic version of vintage Latin. At first listen, "Bolero" sounds like the real article, a heart-wrenching ballad of unrequited love. But when Echeverri savagely sings the tune's chorus, you realize this is not your grandparents' bolero you are listening to:

> *Te dije no más*
> *Y te cagaste de risa*
>
> *I told you no more*
> *You were shitting your pants with laughter*

The opening "Florecita rockera" (Little Rock Flower) was a potent slice of garage punk, and Aterciopelados became a huge success in Colombia. The breakthrough came in 1996 with *La pipa de la paz* (The Pipe of Peace), a more sophisticated effort produced by former Roxy Music guitarist Phil Manzanera, who had expressed the desire to honor his South American roots by working with a group from Colombia.

Recorded in London, *La pipa* showcased Buitrago's strong compositional skills as well as Echeverri's haunting vocals—they could sound manly at times, but also bewitching and feminine. Echeverri had attitude to spare.

The album's opening track, "Cosita seria" (Serious Little Thing), threatened with imminent castration insensitive macho Latinos who issue catcalls at ladies in the streets. "Expreso Amazonia" (Amazon Express) was Buitrago's darkly humorous way of inviting gringos to come over for an eye-opening visit to the Amazon jungle.

> *Llame ya*
> *Echese un mico al hombro*
> *Caliéntese con la fiebre amarilla*
> *Vuelva a sentirse virgen*

> *Call now*
> *Put a monkey on your shoulder*
> *Warm yourself up with a bit of yellow fever*
> *Feel like a virgin again*

But the record's most subversive moment was "La culpable" (The Guilty One), Andrea's declaration of independence disguised as a quaint, string-heavy Colombian *joropo*. The contrast between such a reverential traditional folk song and Echeverri's tough feminist rhetoric was perverse and strangely poignant. While promoting the album to the media, she was questioned ad infinitum about the section of the song in which she expressed her feelings about motherhood.

> *No quiero sentar cabeza*
> *Con un varón, con un varón*
> *No dañaré mi silueta*
> *Con un bebé, con un nené*

> *I don't want to settle down*
> *With no man, no man*
> *I will not ruin my shape*
> *With a baby, a child*

But *La pipa* also showcased the sunny idealism for which Aterciopelados would soon be known (particularly after the positivist statement of *Gozo poderoso*). One of the collection's most melodic tunes, "Buena estrella" (Good Star) countered with good vibrations the gossip and bad wishes that the duo had begun to unleash in its homeland as a result of its considerable success. And "Música," the thunderous, juvenile rock anthem with which Aterciopelados would launch its shows for the next few years, was a simple celebration of the power of music to cleanse the soul.

That same year, Aterciopelados participated in an ill-fated Latin rock tribute to Queen. The resulting album was an embarrassing affair, with appalling versions of "Another One Bites the Dust" by Argentina's Illya Kuryaki and the Valderramas and the venerable "Bohemian Rhapsody" by Mexican quartet Molotov.

Aterciopelados saved the day, delivering the collection's most respectable entry: a pared-down, tuneful cover of 1980's "Play the Game." Sure, the original's endearing synthesizer intro was missing, but Echeverri's serene vocalizing and faithful translation of the lyrics did a remarkable job at preserving the spirit of the original.

In 1998, Aterciopelados was ready for the release of its masterpiece. *Caribe atómico* (Atomic Caribbean) came out one year after the release of the Cadillacs' *Fabulosos calavera* and a year before Café Tacvba's *Revés/Yosoy*.

At the time, Echeverri had fallen head over heels in love with the burgeoning trip-hop movement. She spoke with admiration about groups such as Portishead, Massive Attack, Esthero, and Lamb. So the duo decided to seek out a new producer. They were fortunate enough to find Andrés Levín—the most visionary Latin rock producer after Gustavo Santaolalla, a talented Venezuelan musician with an exquisite taste for lounge and electronica.

The album was recorded in New York and Bogotá. Levín played a variety of instruments, and invited some of his friends from the New York avant-garde music scene to the sessions: Marc Ribot, Vinicius Cantuaria, and Arto Lindsay. Salsa violinist Alfredo de la Fe performed on a couple of tracks. There was also bandoneón, trumpet, and plenty of scratches and samples. All at the service of the best collection of songs that Buitrago and Echeverri had ever written.

A bossa nova record cloaked in velvety electronica, *Caribe* brims with ambiguous melodic lines and oblique loops. Aterciopelados seem to be in no hurry to rock 'n' roll. The lyrics, eloquent observations on themes such as ecology and the deception of physical beauty, float hypnotically over the quiet soundscapes. The aftertaste is cool and sensuous.

Furthermore, *Caribe* went beyond being a mere trip-hop *en español* experiment. The electronica element was loud and clear, but it was counterbalanced by an increased presence of the band's Latin roots (a salsa piano line here, a samba rhythm there), as well as a touch of lounge exotica that gave the mix an irresistibly elegant appeal.

In "Doctora corazón," the mere mention of South America conjures up an acoustic guitar and violin that evoke the soulfulness of Latin music.

> *Se despide esperanzada*
> *De algún lugar de Sudamérica*
>
> *She bids farewell, ever so hopeful*
> *From somewhere in South America*

On the sinuous "Reacio" (Reluctant), Echeverri continued having fun with the *femme fatale* archetypes that are ever ingrained in the Latino subconscious.

> *No huyas de mí, no soy la viuda negra*
> *Y si decido devorarte*
> *Te aseguro te gustará*

> *Don't run away from me, I'm not the black*
> *   widow*
> *Should I decide to devour you*
> *I can assure you will enjoy it*

Caribe atómico may lack the exuberance of *La pipa de la paz*, but it is a perfectly crafted album that underscores the creative peak that *rock en español* was enjoying during the late nineties. With it, Echeverri became the unequivocal priestess of the Latin rock ritual.

Much like Tacvba's *Revés/Yosoy* tour, Aterciopelados' live performances in support of *Caribe* showcased the metamorphosis of a band. A sold-out concert at Los Angeles's six-thousand-seat Greek Theatre was a lesson in how changing a few things about a band's sound can dramatically alter the end result. In this case, replacing a drummer whose playing was a little too heavy for the group and adding electronic drum loops as the backbone for most of the songs gave them a fleshier sound.

The geeky Echeverri was a bit of a fashion dadaist. She appeared wearing a platinum blonde wig, a tight T-shirt with the face of Botticelli's Venus, and a bizarre, silver-colored appendage to her skirt that was meant to simulate a mermaid's tail. She violently tossed the wig away during the rollicking "Música," a transcendent image that still lingers in my mind.

Although the audience clamored for hits such as "Bolero falaz" and "Florecita rockera," the night belonged to songs from *Caribe*. Ironically, the use of electronica had brought a new sense of warmth to the band's stage presence.

Reviewing the show for the *Los Angeles Times*, I concluded:

The most unlikely of pairs, the eccentric Echeverri and the introspective Buitrago have achieved a musical state of grace that is rare among rock bands. They have struck the perfect balance between rock 'n' roll tradition and experimental avant garde. No matter what path they choose to follow next, their influence on Latin music is already incalculable.

In 2001, *Gozo poderoso* came out, and many observers believed that the time had finally come for the band to break into the American mainstream. If *Caribe* was all about Echeverri's love affair with trip-hop, *Gozo* emphasized Colombia's potent kaleidoscope of native rhythms over Anglo pop idioms.

"I love trip-hop," Echeverri told me a couple of months before the *Tonight Show* appearance. "But there comes a time when you need to turn the outside influences off and focus on the music that's playing inside of you."

The record's twelve songs resonated with subtle echoes of salsa, cumbia, and *vallenato*, enhanced by lyrics that accentuated the positive and examined the miracle of love with wide-eyed optimism. Unlike the more solid *Caribe*, *Gozo* relied on a myriad of precious details to create an impression of bittersweet eclecticism: the campy lounge effects of "El album," the Andean flutes at the end of "Rompecabezas" (Puzzle), and the tribal call-and-response chorus of "La misma tijera" (The Same Scissors) underscored the haunting, serene vocals of Echeverri.

"Colombia is going through such a difficult moment right now, that we wanted to make a record to give people hope and make them feel good about our country," the singer told me. Besides producing the entire album themselves, the duo used local musicians only, and enlisted fifteen Colombian artists to create the gorgeous images that adorn *Gozo*'s packaging. "The idea is to use our own success to generate good things around us. Not only musically, but in other disciplines, too."

Caribe had sold a paltry twenty thousand copies in the United States. The release of *Gozo* saw a number of record label executives betting to themselves that Aterciopelados could now woo the same U.S. consumers who favored pop-rock acts such as Dido and Stereolab, or crossover global artists like Brazilian diva Bebel Gilberto.

"My initial expectation is to at least double the amount [sic] of what they sold on the last album," said Jerry Blair, the executive vice president with Arista. "But I won't be happy until we win a Gold record—and possibly a Grammy. What's incredible about the universal language of music is that it touches your soul, regardless of the language it's in. I took a number of executives to see the band live, and everyone left the show mesmerized. So, we are focusing on the music and coming up with a universal game plan."

The band itself was not as optimistic. "They always tell us the same thing," Buitrago told me when I related to him my conversation with Blair. "Every time we come up with a new record, they tell us that this is going to be the one, that they're going to do this and that with it. And we already know nothing's really going to happen. They'll probably be telling us the same thing the next time around, too."

"At least it's nice to see the record company excited about our product," Echeverri interjected. "It's good to see that they want to put some effort into it."

The culmination of this effort was the *Tonight Show* appearance. But the band did nothing to change its music and make the transition into American territory any smoother (performing the Queen cover would have been a way to create some identification with an audience who's not particularly used to listening to music in Spanish). When Leno announced the band's name and Aterciopelados began playing the first notes of "Luz Azul," you could easily see that the live audience was not connecting with the duo. There was an eerie stillness in the air, as if a band from Mars had descended on a television studio in front of an unsuspecting middle America. Echeverri kept her eyes closed during most of the performance, a touch that made her look weirder than usual on the actual telecast.

By the end of 2004, *Gozo* had sold about seventy thousand copies in the United States. When Aterciopelados' next album, the greatest hits collection *Evolución*, came out in 2003, it was released by BMG Latin. The Anglo divisions of the major labels had already lost interest in the Colombian group.

Echeverri: *Héctor and I made a terrible couple, but we were very good friends and had many things in common. Our rela-*

tionship works much better on this level. It was music that brought us together to begin with. Right after we met, we started playing songs. Music is the one thing that has kept us together.

To me, Colombia represents my home and a very small circle of friends. When you are in a band, you're always rehearsing, recording, or playing live. For the last couple of years, it's been very nice. But we also spent many years completely broke, living like the majority of people, I guess.

Colombia is a very conservative country. It's difficult to find space for creativity, for artistic expressions that are truly original. Héctor and I struggled for a long time. We played in bars, I shared a ceramics studio with a couple of friends, stuff like that.

Little by little we created our own space in music, until Aterciopelados sort of exploded. Since then, we've been working, traveling, and also having a lot of fun. We've performed in so many places. Colombia is a very big country and much of it is jungle territory. Plus, rock 'n' roll is an urban sort of thing. We've been to small cities, but not to villages or anything like that.

If anything, my insecurity keeps getting worse. As you become more and more . . . "important," so to speak, you get more scared. Because inside, you're still the same person you were before you became famous. It's an inner thing, because we've experienced a very magical energy, a great connection with the audience from the first time we started playing our music together. So, it's an inner struggle for me. You record an album and you have to hear yourself sing, you have to face the errors you make . . . although you do it with love and you give the best of you, there's still moments when you are going to feel like you're really dumb. Then I find myself thinking: "Maybe I should be a bilingual secretary" or something like that.

❧

In 2005, Echeverri returned to action with a self-titled solo album and a sweeter outlook on life.

"The first couple of Aterciopelados albums were definitely seeped in anger," she told me during a Saturday morning conversation held at the headquarters of Nacional Records, the independent boutique label owned by Latin rock manager Tomás Cookman that released her solo venture. "Then things got better with the man that I eventually chose as my partner. So much, in fact, that we ended up having a baby."

The baby is already a three-year-old toddler, but Echeverri's exhilarating feelings about her pregnancy and the birth of her daughter are at the core of the new album. The collection is divided into *canciones de cama* (bedroom songs) for Echeverri's husband and *canciones de cuna* (lullabies) for her baby.

"Unique artists like Andrea come around only so often," Cookman e-mailed me when I asked him about his decision to work with the singer. "When she was able to get out of her major label contract, I felt that the time was right to sign her. Andrea being available was one of the biggest reasons that I started this label sooner than later."

Echeverri's solo excursion does not signify the breakup of Aterciopelados. In fact, her solo album was produced by Buitrago. But the collection's earthy simplicity and sparse instrumentation suggest a different sound. Tunes such as the lilting "Imán" (Magnet), which includes a vocal cameo by Echeverri's mother, evoke the carefree spirit of kids' music.

"I never studied music, so my songs have always been simple by nature," she explained. "As a little girl, I took some guitar lessons and I've been using what I learned since then. With Aterciopelados, it was Héctor who made things more complex by using his studio expertise and adding dissonant solos or bizarre effects."

Echeverri's songwriting skills may be simple, but her singing is anything but. She can purr seductively on the upbeat numbers, then express infinite longing on the ballads. And she's a natural, having learned how to sing by listening to her mother.

"We have the same way of producing sounds by adding a bit of vibration to the throat," she added. After years of singing professionally, she took singing lessons with two different teachers, but the experience left her disenchanted. "The first teacher told me that I had been doing everything wrong and knew nothing about singing. The second one was a true rebel who believed that you may sing with your toe if you so wish. I took some advice from both and continued singing the way I felt worked for me."

Understandably, considering the new album is all about the freeing effects of motherhood, Echeverri's voice sounds more liberated than ever before. And she has infused the new songs with a playful sense of humor. By describing the process of breastfeeding in concrete lyrics laced with delicious irony, "Lactochampeta" delivers a hilarious satire of Colombian *champeta*, an ever-popular folk genre marked by its obscene lyrical content.

"I'm still outraged by those *champeta* songs, so I thought it would be great to answer with my own take on them," she laughed. "But the greatest thing about that song is that it was my first musical collaboration with [husband] José Manuel Jaramillo, who produced the track with me."

The couple is planning to continue this collaboration with a collection of children's songs. At the same time, Echeverri is recording an album with her mother performing traditional boleros. There's also an Héctor Buitrago solo disc in the horizon (which may be instrumental), as well as the next Aterciopelados record.

"We've written a number of Aterciopelados songs, but we don't have a unifying concept yet," she told me. "The delays brought on by my solo disc were actually positive, since they allowed me to spend time with my daughter and develop parallel projects."

Echeverri was even forced to perform without Buitrago recently, enlisting a female bassist for a gig in the Colombian countryside. The usually introverted Buitrago was busy participating in a local reality show, a decision that Echeverri is still puzzled about.

"I have no idea why he decided to do this," she told me when I asked her about Buitrago's motives. "I understand that as part of this reality show he has to starve and demonstrate his athletic prowess. But I haven't seen the show myself. I don't even own a television."

Caifanes/Jaguares

© Marusa Reyes

Bienvenido a tu ritual.
Este es tu concierto, tu ceremonia.
Vamos a volar, vamos a viajar.

Welcome to your ritual.
This is your concert, your ceremony.
Let's fly, let's travel together.

MOST BANDS SPEND their whole career trying to compose the ultimate rock 'n' roll anthem. Saúl Hernández, the leader of Mexican group Jaguares, seems to churn them out by the dozen.

I met Hernández for the first time late one night in the sterile lobby of a hotel in Beverly Hills (Jaguares was on their 1999 promotional tour). He greeted me with a wide smile and sat his tall, lanky frame on a couch opposite me. It only took a couple of minutes for his Zen-like tranquility to fill the space we occupied. Hernández's long hair, innocent eyes, and permanently placid expression gave him an angelic air. It was easy to understand now why Mexican youth from age fifteen to twenty-five love him like a god—an immensely vulnerable, forgiving, and inviting god.

We talked about "Hoy" (Today), the crunchy slice of mood rock that opens Jaguares' second album, the double *Bajo el azul de tu misterio* (Under the Blue Shade of Your Mystery). The record includes one disc of new material and a second disc recorded in concert. "I started writing that song when I heard that [Mexican poet] Octavio Paz had passed away," he said. "His death left me with an unpleasant feeling. And I didn't intend to write a song about his loss. But I did write about how volatile life can be. *Hoy te velaré.* Today

I will mourn you. It was a way of capturing the moment when somebody is going away, and I mean that in all its possible meanings. Going away as in death, but also through meditation, finding a new path, or dreaming or experiencing a new emotion. A going away that can also be seen as a liberation of sorts. I strove to preserve a feeling of fragility in that song."

In a way, this man has built an entire career out of his ability to convey fragility, for which his adolescent fans adore him.

Hernández's stardom didn't begin with Jaguares. The band is actually the continuation of Caifanes, the group that, together with Argentina's Soda Stereo, ushered in the second coming of Latin rock. You could say that Jaguares is a more mature version of Caifanes, with longer songs and more intricate sonic textures.

Stylistically, Jaguares takes as a starting point the dark guitar textures of eighties British groups such as the Cure, marrying them to a notoriously Mexican sensibility. Tunes like the nostalgic "Detrás de los cerros" (Beneath the Hills), from Jaguares' debut, are shimmering new pages in the Latin American songbook, yet could not have existed without the influence of Anglo pop.

"When the whole 'dark' or gothic movement came to Mexico from England, it was nothing new to us," Hernández explained. "We already had a dark aesthetic of our own. OK, it didn't originate in London. But if you study the bolero lyrics, you'll see that there's some pretty sad stuff there. Songs that talk about unrequited love, abandonment, and endless weeping. Generally, the lyrics don't talk about death. They talk about being left by the person you loved, about being able to survive the pain. We have a taste for the bitter, and that's part of what makes us passionate people. We also have a very ironic stance toward death. We even have a day for it, *el día de los muertos*, where we go to the graves of our loved ones and leave them plates of the food they liked to eat. I hope I never stray away from all that. It's one of the links in the chain of my life that I would like to maintain intact."

Hernández: *Like all of my deepest desires, the birth of Caifanes came straight from the heart. I started the band on my own, which explains why to this day Jaguares feels like a very intimate and personal affair to me.*

The first member was Diego Herrera, with whom I sat down to write Caifanes' first songs ("Mátenme porque me muero" [Kill Me Because I'm Dying], "Será por eso" [It Will Be Because of This]). Then we invited Sabo [Romo], and finally Alfonso [André]. Our first show took place in Rock-otitlán, the one venue where everybody wanted to play back then. After playing in a number of other underground clubs, we were lucky to meet an Argentine producer, Oscar López, who happened to be looking for rock bands to sign with the BMG Latin label. He talked to us and signed us on the spot. It was like a Hollywood script.

We weren't successful right away, something about which I feel extremely grateful now. We learned how to live with our music under the worst possible circumstances, which gave us strength and prepared us for our eventual metamorphosis. After releasing our first album, we came out with the single of "La negra Tomasa" [Black Tomasa] with "La bestia humana" [The Human Beast] as its b-side. That record sold a million copies and introduced Caifanes to a massive new audience. Thank God it took a long time for all of it to happen.

❧

"La negra Tomasa" is actually a new version of the Cuban classic "Bilongo" reworked as a cumbia and performed by a rock band.

"I started by questioning the relationship between a man and a woman," Hernández told me. "And analyzing Mexican people, our idiosyncrasy, the way our society works. Still within the framework of a dialogue between a couple. I always try to have two separate realities coexisting in my songs. One is the immediate reality, the one you perceive right away. And the other one is more subtle, underlying; something that might be discovered later on."

Hernández's mixture of the Latin and the Anglo found its perfect vehicle in "La célula que explota" (The Exploding Cell), a tune off 1990's *El diablito* (Little Devil)—an album that is as close to a rock 'n' roll ranchera as Mexican music has ever known. At the time, the culture clash engineered by Hernández seemed breathtakingly fresh.

"Up to a certain extent, 'La célula' ended up competing with 'La negra Tomasa,'" he explained. "After doing a cumbia, I didn't want to repeat myself and do another one, although the business side of popular music certainly welcomes repetition. I decided to explore my *mariachi* influences, which ended up being all over the song. The trumpets at the end, for instance. The ballad side of it. It was all about our identity as Mexicans. We're not a *mariachi* group, but we can do something like this."

By the mid-nineties, the singer had disbanded Caifanes, and his songwriting became more concerned with texture, re-creating the epic pathos of arena-rock artists such as Pink Floyd and late-period the Cure. A particularly vivid dream became the basis for Jaguares. "The name refers to the warrior within me that emerged during the difficult transition from Caifanes to the new band," he explained. "In pre-Hispanic cultures, the jaguar represents the most powerful being in creation, a god that transforms itself into other creatures and is able to switch from one reality to the other." And on a more metaphysical note: "If you kill a jaguar, cut him open, and spread his skin on the ground, it looks like the representation of a cosmic map. Every one of its spots, a galaxy."

Jaguares' first album, *El equilibrio de los jaguares* (The Jaguars' Balance), came out in 1996. Produced by Don Was, it was a sumptuous recording, including tracks that quickly became *rock en español* standards: "Dime jaguar" (Tell Me, Jaguar), "Imagíname" (Imagine Me), and "Las ratas no tienen alas" (Rats Have No Wings). Hernández was beginning to create a mythology of darkness that later albums have only enhanced.

The singer has certainly experienced his share of troublesome moments. At the age of nine, he lost his mother to a horrible disease, an event that might explain the aching wistfulness of his music. Once he became a rock star, he developed benign tumors on his throat that placed his vocal chords in serious danger, forcing him to undergo surgery twenty-four times.

"The tumors don't hurt, because the affected muscles are very tiny, without nerve endings in them," Hernández explained. "More than pain, you get a choking feeling. When the tumors were really big, it became difficult to breathe. And if you don't take care of yourself, it can reach the point where you need a tracheotomy. This is one of those tests that life sends your way."

When his raspy voice failed him during a concert in Mexico some years ago, Hernández found comfort in his fans, who came to his aid. Instead of interrupting the show, he continued playing the guitar, watching as thousands of people sang every word of his songs.

"One doctor told me that my tumors were psychosomatic. I don't know what to say to that," he told me. "Now I go to vocal therapy every three months, and everything appears to be under control."

Hernández: *My mother used to say to me, "La lucha es diaria y a cada instante" (We struggle on a daily basis and during every single moment of our lives). Implying you should never stop fighting. I think that saying had a profound impact on me. Your attitude toward life defines everything. You define your own road, day by day.*

I also think that coming to terms with the things that happened to me made me the person that I am today. I have learned a lot from my misfortune. On reflection, I still think that life has given me more than it has taken away. My mother's death was one of the most important things that ever happened to me. I feel the repercussions of that event, even today. But I can't get angry about it. I can't get angry about something that's completely out of my control. If I walk through life causing my own misfortune, then the mistake is all mine. But if I walk through life and misfortune just happens, there's nothing I can do about it but accept it.

No matter how hard you are hit, there's always a way out. People can harm you, bend you, beat you up, step on you, and spit on you, but they can never touch your soul. Once, many years ago, when I wasn't well known yet, I was brutally beaten by a few Mexican policemen. Back then, if you were young and your hair was long, you were considered a criminal. These policemen were convinced that I carried drugs with me, and they hit me on the head with the back of a gun. I was lying on the ground, and I told them: "You can hit me as much as you want, but you'll never be able to touch me." At that moment, they stopped beating me and left.

That story is an example of how I see life. How I deal with death, with betrayal, with disease. Life is very sad, and once in a while it throws you down. What doesn't kill you, though, will probably make you stronger.

Jaguares' third album came out in 2001. *Cuando la sangre galopa* (When Blood Gallops) is probably the band's most fully realized work, thanks to the densely layered guitar riffs and the messianic sincerity of Hernández's paper-thin voice. He uses a Cuban *tumbao* ("Como tú"—Like You) or a son jarocho *guitarrón* ("La vida no es igual"—Life Is Not the Same) not as cute stylistic rip-offs, but as textural additions to his morbid palette of mysterious grays, bloody reds, and the darkest of blues. Dark and theatrical, this is FM-friendly rock of the highest order.

Its follow-up, 2003's *El primer instinto* (The First Instinct), was *La Sangre*'s counterpart, an airy, semi-acoustic collection that found the singer selecting choice cuts from the Caifanes and Jaguares songbooks and reinventing them through the addition of a *mariachi* ensemble, a salsa orchestra (Mexico's venerable La Sonora Santanera), and a string ensemble conducted by Beck's father, David Campbell. *El primer* is a fun record that revels in the band's Mexican roots.

Hernández: *I always feel watched when I come to Los Angeles. Everybody's an actor here, everybody belongs to some kind of clique, even the person who drives the garbage truck.*

That's one of the reasons why I enjoy going to the jungle and spending time with the Lacandones Indians so much. I stay with them for a while, and I learn a lot. There's a wisdom, an air of peace about them—I reckon it's having survived for so many years. On a genetic level, they must have accumulated an impressive strength. And because of their long history, they possess a millennia-old wisdom. Consequently, their cosmology is very different than ours.

Right now, I see the world as being in a very strange state of putrefaction. Societies all over the planet are decomposing. That's why I try to make music that reflects peace. As a songwriter, I want to seduce my audience into a more positive outlook. The worst moment of your life might also be the best one. Maybe we should accept the bad times as a purifying experience.

Once, I was leaving the camp of the Lacandones for a brief trip to Mexico City, and I asked one of my friends there if he needed anything. "I'll be back in a couple of days," I told him. "Is there anything you need from the city?" He stood there, looked at the trees and back to me, and said: "Nothing. I don't need anything."

I actually got married in the jungle. Don Antonio, the last carrier of the mystical tradition of the Lacandones, performed

© Marusa Reyes

the ceremony. It was beautiful. The only thing he requested was that we didn't take any pictures. He emanated a sense of peace and light. Sitting down with him, watching him laugh, watching his eyes, was a very pleasant experience. They also maintain a relationship with nature that we have already lost. Their contact with that instinctive language is very strong. We see a fly on the wall and smash it with a stick. They would probably carry on a conversation with it.

A few months before the release of *El primer instinto*, I met with the members of Jaguares outside a Hollywood hotel and we drove together in a van to the Arrowhead Pond in Anaheim, where the group was performing a sold-out show sharing the spotlight with Morrissey.

Looking placid as always, Hernández sat next to me and showed me video images of his baby daughter that he had uploaded onto his laptop. The computer also contained tracks from the yet unreleased new album. He gave me some headphones and played track after track, curious to see what I thought of them. He was really proud of the new work, proud of his decision to stick to an acoustic format and present his favorite songs with minimal arrangements.

Throughout concerts and album releases, Hernández had already seen me many times and treated me as a friend. When we got to the arena, he guided me backstage, found a place for me to sit and, later in the afternoon, took me to the catering area himself and made sure that I had something to eat. I've been sweet talked before by plenty of musicians in search of good press—but Hernández's kindness has always been transparent and devoid of any ulterior motives. That day, he treated everyone who crossed his path with equal generosity, from his fellow band members and their families to the fans and the many workers who make a concert possible.

The band was curious about meeting Morrissey (the Smiths had been an inevitable reference for Caifanes—and the acts now share a large number of similarly minded fans) but news arrived from the Morrissey camp that the British singer was to remain in his dressing room until the performance, after which he was to be whisked back to Los Angeles. Hernández appeared slightly puzzled by this *mysterioso* rock star attitude, but his expression showed no signs of negativity. Instead, he sat down with the other Jaguares and played a couple of riffs on the guitar. Some of the sounds reminded me of *Red*, a seventies album by British group King Crimson, and I asked them if they had heard the record. Two of them began singing a heavy, Crimson-esque riff at the same time. I asked guitarist Vampiro if he had enjoyed his stint with famous pop-rockers Maná. He looked down, smiling, making it clear that he was much happier being a Jaguar.

I walked to the arena and was surprised to see how packed it was. This was an unusually large crowd for a *rock en español* performance. Jaguares had made it without sacrificing an ounce of integrity. The show was trademark Hernández, dark and epic, punctuated by Alfonso André's punchy drumming and the singer's fervent communication with the audience. It ended, as many Jaguares shows do, with a *mariachi* ensemble performing traditional *rancheras* ("El Rey," for instance) to the enthusiastic applause of the young audience.

As soon as the concert was over, I ran backstage. Hernández was putting his guitar away, a beatific smile on his face. He gave me a hug and I suddenly felt a tremendous energy emanating from him, like a surge of electricity. I commented on this and he laughed. "Can't you see?" he said. "It's the audience. It's the love that they give me."

Gustavo Cerati

OUR STORY BEGINS in the early nineties, on a night when Gustavo Cerati happened to be in London and went to see the Orb in concert. That evening occupies a special place in Latin music, because it was then that Cerati discovered electronica and the spirit of *rock en español* was forever changed.

At the time, Cerati was still the singer, guitarist, and songwriter of Soda Stereo—the first group to achieve massive success by bringing rock into the mainstream throughout Latin America.

Soda was a child of the eighties. Formed by Cerati, bassist Zeta Bosio, and drummer Charly Alberti, the Buenos Aires trio was blindly infatuated with British new wave. Early hits—1985's "Nada personal" (Nothing Personal) comes immediately to mind—had the quirky, hummable choruses and flat sonics that defined the zeitgeist of the moment in England, from the Cure and Joy Division to Human League and Spandau Ballet. Soda Stereo strove to be the Latino version of all those groups, and the public responded enthusiastically. Soda became a supergroup, even though most of its early albums are spotty at best. That is, until that night.

"I remember when the Police came to play live in Argentina," Cerati reminisced when we met for coffee in 1999 in a Los Angeles hotel lobby. "They were only three guys, but they had such a big sound. And at the same time, what they did was so simple. I didn't receive such an injection of enthusiasm from music until the electronica scene came to be. I remember that Orb show as a very important moment in my career. It was very psychedelic, but also marked by heavy doses of tongue-in-cheek humor." He was cordial and softspoken, the antithesis of a rock star. His singing voice is not particularly distinctive—even colorless—but there's something mercurial about his personality, let alone his undeniable gift for writing memorable songs.

Back in Buenos Aires, Cerati announced to his incredulous bandmates that he had seen the light. It was the dawn of the computer as a music-making companion, the birth of a million textures. "You have a traditional rock band, and one of its members buys a computer," he explained. "What do the other band members do? Inevitably, there's something a little solitary about the process of making music with a computer. Some people were really upset that I got into electronica, because they didn't perceive it as part of rock culture. If you listen to Pink Floyd's *Dark Side of the Moon*, though, you'll hear many passages that are imbued with electronic music."

Soda Stereo became a new band—the incandescent mantle of electronica gave Cerati's simplistic pop melodies an air of sumptuous elegance. The change became apparent in 1992's *Dynamo*, the highly dramatic album that featured "Luna roja" (Red Moon) and "Sweet sahumerio."

By the time Soda released its gorgeous swan song, 1995's *Sueño stereo* (Stereo Dream), the shimmering textures of ambient dominated the album's finale, a trilogy of tracks that took you from the sinuous psychedelia of "Planta" (complete with a string quartet) to the ethereal instrumental "X-Playo" and "Moiré"—a trippy, near catatonic closing song that stands to this day as one of Zeta Bosio's favorite Soda moments. The album began auspiciously with "Ella usó mi cabeza como un revólver" (She Used My Head Just Like a Gun), which combined a strong Beatles influence with classic Soda guitars. "Paseando por Roma" (Riding in Rome) was another highlight, an exhilarating pop song with a propulsive vibe that evoked the joys of exotic traveling.

"I was thinking about that the other day," Cerati commented in 1999. "Why did we use Rome as a place? We've never been to Rome. We were listening to the song, and felt that it gave us the image of somebody riding a motorbike in the streets of Rome. But I'm also talking about us in that song when I say:

He cambiado, pero mi corazón permanece intacto

I've changed, but my heart remains the same

"When groups are about to split up, they become self-referential," he added with a laugh. "I warn you, when a band starts talking about itself, that's it. I think that in general, when you start talking about yourself a lot, something's about to change."

Before breaking up the band, Cerati had experienced a self-imposed exile in Chile and recorded two oblique solo albums that further emphasized his fascination with technology: 1992's *Colores santos* (Saintly Colors), a collaboration with Latintronica pioneer Daniel Melero, and 1993's excellent *Amor amarillo* (Yellow Love). The band's end was inevitable. The trio was plagued by the same problems that destroyed the Police: Zeta and Charly were at the core of Soda's distinctive sound—but the songs, vocals, and guitars were all Cerati's. He got all the songwriting credit and publishing monies. He could afford to leave the band any day he pleased. The other two couldn't.

Cerati: *I guess my favorite Soda Stereo albums are the last three ones. I think it's really good when that happens, when*

you like the last albums of a band instead of the first ones. Hopefully the later records are the product of an evolution.

By the time we made Sueño Stereo, *I was already listening to a lot of instrumental music. I didn't want to do just songs anymore. Zeta was always behind me as far as these musical adventures went. Charly was more in the background. With that, I don't mean that he boycotted my ideas, but I think he didn't understand them as much. He understood a record like* Dynamo, *for instance, a long time after we recorded it. I was really exultant about that record. I had discovered something and I wanted to implement it in the group's music.*

I wasn't sure of the results I would get, but that last sequence of three songs in the album was definitely planned. It was the ideal moment for a suite to come in and bring an end to the record. I thought that it was very interesting that a group like ours could afford the luxury to take risks like that. I also saw the group as a kind of antenna, absorbing all sorts of musical influences and processing them into our own style.

In any case, Sueño Stereo *was a difficult record for us. Our relationship was undergoing a crisis. The enthusiasm wasn't the same. And we didn't argue over a lot of things, because we didn't even have the energy to do it anymore. We stopped saying what we really felt. I remember how relieved I was to finish it. That was very telling, because usually we felt ecstatic when we were done with an album.*

Soda was in bad shape even before we made Sueño. *I had gone to Chile and recorded* Amor amarillo. *When I came back, everybody was staring at me, like wanting me to pay for it because I had left. And the truth is that by leaving, I had distanced myself from the group. After doing* Dynamo *and changing record companies, I had felt it necessary to do that.*

In the meantime, there was a horrible accident that affected Zeta's family. His two kids were in a car that was hit by a bus and caught fire. One of them died, and Zeta wasn't there when it happened. All this took place when we were in doubt about whether we wanted to carry on as a band. When the accident hit Zeta, it was only natural that we decided to go forward and do another album.

Soda retired in 1997 with a series of concerts that were dutifully captured on tape for the double-CD release *El último concierto* (The Last Concert). Fans and critics bemoaned the singer's apparent coldness. Cerati was the exact opposite of the Cadillacs' Vicentico. While Vicentico will curse and threaten to punch the daylights out of those audience members that annoy him, Cerati keeps his stage patter to a minimum and evokes the same glacial attitude favored by the British rockers he grew up admiring.

Cerati: *Saying goodbye was a very difficult process. Why say goodbye at all? I always thought I would continue making music for the rest of my life anyway. But there were three of us, and we agreed to do the shows. I was against the idea, especially because I didn't want to have to say goodbye several times. When you take your wife to the airport, she only leaves once. Otherwise, the experience of her leaving would lose its impact. In our case, there was no way the fans were going to let us do just one farewell show.*

I also wanted to emphasize the musical side of the show. I wanted to have a dignified goodbye. I couldn't start crying from the very first song. It was too much for me. People in the audience were weeping from beginning to end. . . . I guess my message to the people was that we were always about the music, and that's the way we were going to end. I have an alarm inside of me that deters me from being a crowd pleaser. Even when I was in a stadium with ninety thousand people, I always tried to talk to them in a normal way. I can't submit the masses to my whims and treat them as if I am a popular leader. And I think people appreciate being treated like that.

The demise of Soda Stereo was a cause of consternation for millions of Latin rock fans. But the move was ultimately beneficial, both for Cerati *and* the genre. *Bocanada* (Smoke Puff), Cerati's first solo album after leaving the trio, stands as his finest work to date.

Released in 1999, Cerati's first post-Soda solo effort is a seamless work of pop perfection in which the language of samples, sound effects, and electronic beats flow with mesmerizing fluidity. It was recorded in Cerati's own studio in Vicente López, a picturesque, upper-class Buenos Aires neighborhood blessed with a constant cooling breeze that emanates from a nearby river. Cerati worked alone, then invited a few friends over to record overdubs.

The album begins with "Tabú," a track defined by a carnivalesque sample that combines tribal exuberance with camp, full of noise and abandon. "It's like a jungle thing, but on top of that you have a heroic-sounding tune, almost like a cowboy song," Cerati explained. "I was looking for that sort of explosive contrast." Even more jarring, the title track lifted a snippet of "Eruption," a bombastic tune by seventies Dutch prog-rock group Focus, into nineties operatic pop with a touch of Cerati's hieratic vocal delivery.

But the high point is "Verbo carne" (Flesh Verb), with the London Symphony Orchestra joining in for what sounds like a cross between a James Bond theme song and the mystique of a Massive Attack single. In fact, Massive collaborator Gavin Wright conducted the orchestra on those sessions. "Not a coincidence," smiled Cerati, who counts the seminal *Blue Lines* as a defining album for him.

If Soda Stereo's early albums smacked of imitation, Cerati had grown and learned to incorporate influences into his own life experiences. Samples and all, there's nothing artificial about *Bocanada*. The songs here function as an excuse for reflection. The choruses linger in your head, like the afternoon light slowly fading into the night through an open window.

Cerati: *With* Bocanada, *I understood how to compose a song better, how to be myself, less tortured and obsessive than before. It's been a fifteen-year-long process. Something I discovered recently is the pleasure involved in it . . . how important it is to have the real desire to make a record. When you are with a band, a certain feeling of inertia will be inevitably generated. You do a record, you go on tour. You already know that after that, you'll do another record. After a while, you're not sure about your motives anymore. Are you making a record because you want to, or because you have to?*

In between the Soda Stereo albums I recorded two solo projects. Those side trips taught me a lot about feeling alive musically. And when there's a lot of pleasure involved in the process, I think those records are more likely to stand the test of time. I drew from all those experiences for Bocanada.

The process was like this: first, I recorded the basic tracks in my own home studio. Then, I went to London, where I did the orchestra and some voice overdubs. At home, it was very relaxed. Technology has gotten to a point where you can make a record at home. And it's not because I have a lot of money. It's accessible to anybody. Then, it was nice to take some distance from the material and receive feedback from the British sound engineer. It was like a test. When I was recording in Buenos Aires, I would look through the window and see a sunny street. In London, it was raining and people were walking with their umbrellas. It was a great contrast.

Cerati played the new material on stage in Argentina and other Latin countries. The response was initially grudging, but slowly became increasingly enthusiastic. The fans were willing to give him a chance.

"I was afraid that people would want to hear the old Soda Stereo songs too much. But people came—in Buenos Aires, we sold out six nights at the Gran Rex Theater, which is incredible, considering everybody's broke there," he commented, alluding to the economic crisis that plagued the South American nation.

In Mexico, loyal fans chanted his name and the new material was accepted wholeheartedly, even though Cerati relied on plenty of prerecorded tracks; on "Verbo carne," he crooned over a taped symphony orchestra. "I wanted to give the fans a sonic collage, reproducing the cut-and-paste vibe of my record," he said. "A mixture of blood and machinery."

The electronic bravado of *Bocanada* tempts you to believe that the almighty Soda Stereo may actually have been a stepping-stone for Cerati, on his way to grander heights. A revisionist—and somewhat sacrilegious—approach, I guess. "I'm not about to deny the importance of a given moment," Cerati told me when I suggested the supremacy of his solo career versus Soda's output. "But when I get involved with something, I tend to forget whatever came before it. The truth is that you can't do what's already been done. You have to look forward."

Cerati reached the apex of his art-rock phase on his next project, *Once episodios sinfónicos* (Eleven Symphonic Episodes). Dressed in a flamboyant outfit that vaguely recalled the cape of Saint Exupery's *The Little Prince*, he performed a show at Buenos Aires' venerable Teatro Colón joined by a symphony orchestra. The repertoire included tunes from *Bocanada* and previous solo efforts, as well as a few Soda numbers. The resulting album is as majestic and moody as can be expected. Watching the DVD that accompanied its release, however, you can't help but notice the audience of Argentine fans' bored expressions. *Bocanada*'s mood was textured and experimental, but there was also a lot of humor in it. *Once episodios* had no humor whatsoever. The orchestral arrangements by Alejandro Terán were not that good to begin with. Maybe it was time for Cerati to return to the Soda aesthetic.

Siempre es hoy (Forever Is Today) was released in 2003. A jarring and somewhat disappointing change in style, the record emphasized robotic beats and jangly guitars over mystery and melody. Its abstract, occasionally Teutonic, eighties-fixated motifs made Cerati's voice sound particularly pedestrian.

Lyrically, *Siempre es hoy* functioned as a sentimental confession of sorts, reflecting on Cerati's divorce from Cecilia Amenábar, the mother of his two children, and his newly found domestic bliss with model and singer Deborah De Corral, who contributed backup vocals. But there's little psychological insight on the subject of romantic rebirth beyond the expected poetic ruminations. The record's best track, "Karaoke," is a vicious attack on former wife Amenábar, who at the time had her own television show.

> *Ahora tienes tu propio show*
> *Como un rey vengador*
> *Vengador*
>
> *Now you have your own show*
> *Like a vindictive king*
> *Vindictive*

Still, *Siempre es hoy* is far from being a bad album. Cerati has lost none of his touch for dreaming up deliciously oblique choruses. It's hard to dismiss a record that includes such memorable songs as the sunny, bittersweet "Nací para esto" (I Was Born for This) and the rootsy "Sulky." The latter, a shimmering concoction of crystalline electronics and unadulterated South American folk, shows clearly why Cerati is still an indispensable force in Latin rock. He followed it up with *Reversiones*, a sprawling two-CD set of *Siempre es hoy* remixes done by a number of intriguing DJs and producers. Cerati further delayed the recording of a new solo album by participating in a number of electronica productions such as Roken, a trio he created with Flavio Etcheto and Leandro Fresco.

In 2005, the rumors of a Soda Stereo reunion became increasingly strong, bolstered by the release of the band's first official DVD collection. It would appear that a new album by Latin America's most beloved trio may become a reality sooner than later.

Maldita Vecindad

NOTHING IS QUITE what it seems in the enigmatic world of Maldita Vecindad.

In 2002, the very existence of this seminal group was the subject of endless speculation. Four years had elapsed since the Mexican quintet had released an album—the kaleidoscopic, World-beat friendly *Mostros*—and subsequently severed ties with its longtime label, BMG Latin.

Even though Maldita had toured sporadically since then, it had slowly but steadily ceased to occupy an essential place in the pantheon of *rock en español*—its name replaced by artists like Molotov, El Gran Silencio, and Nortec Collective.

And yet, Maldita was anything but moribund. In fact, its five members had been busier than ever with a dizzying variety of solo projects. "Taking a sabbatical is healthy for a band that has been together for over fifteen years," explained Roco, Maldita's lead singer, from his home in Mexico City. "Otherwise, you run the danger of becoming a merchant instead of an artist."

Of the dozens of ongoing Maldita solo projects, which included forays into electronica, children's music, production work, and even music journalism (the band's former drummer, Pancho, began writing a weekly column for the Mexican newspaper *Reforma*), Roco's stint as a DJ sounded like the most intriguing one. "I don't like the DJ term, though," he was quick to point out. "I prefer the word *sonidero*—the almighty maker of sounds."

Humorously entitled "Cyber Pachucote Sound System," Rocco's DJ sets emphasize the cultural schizophrenia and voracious love of music that defines Maldita's aesthetic to begin with. "I mix up Pérez Prado with James Brown, Tigres del Norte with Fela Kuti, and gypsy music from Hungary," he said gleefully. "I guess that's what we've always tried to do with Maldita anyway—cram all those different styles into one single song."

Maldita did a pretty good job at it. The group's early recordings, particularly the 1991 classic *El circo* (The Circus), were instrumental in creating the lexicon of Latin rock by blending ska, reggae, and punk with *ranchera*, mambo, cumbia, and Mexican *banda*.

El circo was Maldita's second album. It was produced by Gustavo Santaolalla and begins with the hyperkinetic "Pachuco," a symbolic tune that illustrates the dialogue between a young rocker and his father—a former *pachuco*. To this day, the song drives audiences crazy during the group's live shows.

> *Hey pa fuiste pachuco*
> *Tambien te regañaban*
> *Hey pa bailabas mambo*
> *Tienes que recordarlo*
>
> *Hey dad you were a pachuco yourself*
> *You were scolded too*
> *Hey dad you used to dance the mambo*
> *You have to remember*

There's a sense of urgency to *El circo* that Maldita would never be able to capture again on record. Just like the Cadillacs in Argentina, Maldita is inspired by the sounds of ska, transposing its universe into the streets of Mexico City for a number of poignant slice-of-life vignettes.

❧

Roco: *Our defining year was 1994. It signified the death of our romantic notions about the music industry. For the first time in our lives, we realized that there was more to our career than just the music that we were all passionate about. The interests of other people were also involved.*

After El circo *we released a live album,* Pata de perro *(Dog Paw). Then we went to New York and recorded a new album with producer Bill Laswell. That album never saw the light of day—we don't even have the master. It was canned by the label after a change of guard and various disagreements with the band and our producer. For us, it was a defining moment. Much of what we were doing had nothing to do with the industry's vision of us.* El circo *had been pure magic: we did as we pleased, and a year later satisfied the label by selling massive numbers of records. But it wasn't our intention. The label and the media started harboring expectations that were too big for us. We were young. We wanted to continue making good music.*

That 1994 record was highly experimental. The fact that it never came out was a hard blow. We quickly realized that the one area where we could maintain our passion for music intact without being manipulated by the industry was in our live performances. We didn't have the clarity to be conscious about this at the time, but we did find refuge in touring. That was ours and could not be taken away from us. In the meantime, we kept writing songs. In fact, we have about twenty numbers that we have been playing live throughout the years without ever recording them.

In 1998, *Mostros* included "El cocodrilo" (The Crocodile), one of Maldita's most perfectly realized songs. What surprises the most about this song is the loving delicacy with which it's been put together. A standard Maldita hit (like "Pachuco," for instance) is pure rage and energy in motion. An altogether different kind of song, "Cocodrilo" includes a heart-wrenching sax solo and a poetic, salsa sort of keyboard line courtesy of special guest Irving Lara.

Named after the Mexican moniker for taxis in the fifties, "Cocodrilo" is actually an homage to that country's Golden Age of Cinema, when frothy comedies were shot in lavish black and white and the films' musical numbers were just as important as the plot. The lyrics mention some of the most endearing stars of the time, from Juan Orol and Tongolele to the original mambo king Pérez Prado. The tune includes samples of his voice.

"It's a song about the power of memory," Roco told me. "And about the possibility we have of reinventing and remembering our city and its stories just the way they were in the past. Musically, it's an homage to the *mambo* and the *cha cha cha*, all the Afro-Cuban music that has been so very present in the history of Mexico."

The rest of *Mostros* covers more familiar territory, but with a renewed sense of maturity. There's a hidden twelfth track, "Sirena" (Mermaid), in which the group confirms its love affair with North African *rai* music, and a new, revised version of the corrido "El Barzón," about a peasant's decision to rebel against the exploitation of a greedy landowner. The album was helmed by celebrated electronica producer and performer Michael Brook, whose love for fusing disparate cultures certainly fits well with Maldita's ambitious views of what "world music" should really sound like. The band has the rare virtue of making music that retains the essence of Mexico while looking to the world with a joyous sense of lust for new, foreign sounds.

Roco: *Once we released* Mostros *we decided to leave the band aside for a while and explore a number of personal interests. Our deal with the label was over—and we felt overjoyed about that. No more label, no more pressure. We took a sabbatical that lasted almost two years. People around us told us that we were mad to do something like that, but it was healthy for the band. We developed our individual projects and got together to perform shows that were for the most part linked to causes that we support.*

This is an intense moment for Maldita. We love the freedom of making music without any outside expectations. We want to nourish and transform ourselves—and at the same time we want to transform the reality around us through the music. We got together in 2003 with the idea of eventually releasing a new album. In the meantime, our drummer Pacho decided to leave the band. He had been with us from the beginning, and his departure was yet another change that we needed some time to process.

When we started out, most Latin rock bands were not into the fusion of genres that we favor. Back then, the concept of underscoring your own cultural roots as a departure for these musical fusions was not trendy yet. Lyrically, there were few bands like us, offering a reflection on social and political issues.

Once El circo came out, the movement grew in popularity. Suddenly, there were bands from Mexico and other Latin American countries, even Europe and the United States, that jumped on that bandwagon. Many of those groups got the Grammy awards and the record sales. But I don't really mind. Throughout our career, I remain stunned by the credibility that Maldita Vecindad has enjoyed among the Latin rock fans and the specialized press.

It remains to be seen whether Maldita can recapture the zeitgeist of the moment with a new album. "It's true that we haven't received a huge amount of recognition from the Latin music industry," mused Roco without a hint of bitterness in his voice. "Then again, the music industry is not a cultural academy. It's driven by commercial interests. On the other hand, I feel that Maldita has been recognized and honored by the Latin rock movement itself. I feel deeply moved by the fact that we keep meeting emerging bands that name us openly as an important influence—like the whole L.A. Chicano rock wave."

He paused for a moment, then added: "That's where we belong, really. In the streets. We're engaged in a never-ending dialogue with the heart of this movement."

Fito Páez

AT HIS BEST, Fito Páez is one of the most talented singer/song-writers Latin rock has ever seen, a bluesy piano man who can effortlessly switch from sunny Beatlesque harmonies to shadowy tango moods. Think of Páez as the Elton John of Argentine rock—but with a Latino's gift for expressing the contradictions of life in a third-world country through lyrics of incisive poetry.

Born in the provincial city of Rosario, Páez moved to Buenos Aires in 1982, recording with Argentine rockers Juan Carlos Baglietto and Charly García. Two years later, he released *Del 63* (Born in '63), a rustic and highly sentimental debut. His following record, 1985's *Giros* (Turns), included an instant classic: "11 y 6," a heartbreaking narrative detailing the romance between two street children who meet in the gray streets of Buenos Aires.

> *Se escondieron en el centro*
> *Y en el baño de un bar*
> *Sellaron todo con un beso*

> *They hid together downtown*
> *And in the bathroom of a bar*
> *They sealed their relationship with a kiss*

Ciudad de pobres corazones (City of Poor Hearts), released in 1987, was a seminal record, expressing Páez's profound rage and despondence after his grandmother and aunt were gruesomely murdered the year before. The title track, a rock anthem of anger and revulsion, is particularly apocalyptic.

> *En esta puta ciudad todo se incendia y se va*
> *Matan a pobres corazones*

En esta sucia ciudad no hay que seguir ni parar
Ciudad de locos corazones

In this fucking city everything burns up and goes
They're killing those poor hearts
In this dirty city you can't stop nor keep going
The city of crazy hearts

The singer was reborn psychologically when he met and fell in love with actress Cecilia Roth. He poured his renewed faith in life and romance into 1992's *El Amor después del amor* (Love after Love), one of the most satisfying Latin rock records of the nineties. Filled with hummable songs that made one think of Páez as a distant cousin of Paul McCartney, *El amor* became a commercial juggernaut in *rock en español* terms, selling over 650,000 copies. The album's guest artists include a coterie of Argentina's finest, from Charly García and Luis Alberto Spinetta (both of whom strongly influenced Páez's own career), to Andrés Calamaro, Claudia Puyó, and folk guitarist Lucho González. Celeste Carballo and Fabiana Cantilo (Páez's former flame) sang together on the funky "Dos días en la vida" (Two Days in a Lifetime), an homage to the Ridley Scott film *Thelma and Louise*. Páez even invited veteran folk songstress Mercedes Sosa to contribute vocals on the soulful "Detrás del muro de los lamentos" (Behind the Wall of Grief). He would later produce one of Sosa's own records, a collaboration that would end in a complete fracas. Songs such as the dramatic "Tumbas de la gloria" (Tombs of Glory) and the optimistic "A rodar la vida" (Let Life Roll) are, to this day, obligatory staples in Páez's live shows.

Páez's follow-up was 1994's *Circo beat*, an album that felt like warmed up leftovers from the *El amor* sessions. *Euforia,*

released in 1996, was almost depressing—a noticeably anemic unplugged session that included old favorites and a couple of new originals.

Enemigos íntimos (Intimate Enemies) was released in 1998,
an unusual collaboration with Spain's *enfant terrible* Joaquín
Sabina. The album title, unfortunately, was somewhat
prophetic. In it, Páez sang and toyed with various keyboards
and samples, whereas Sabina lent his deep voice and bohemian
attitude to the mix. Composed by both artists, the songs are
filled with literary and pop-culture references, as in the breezy,
angst-ridden "Si volvieran los dragones" (If Dragons Returned).
The cool "Lázaro" is an opportunity for Sabina to create one
of his trademark moods of solitary contemplation, whereas
"Cecilia," a hyperrealistic love poem set to a lushly orchestrated
ballad, finds Páez in love with the very notion of love.

Moments of old fashioned magic abound throughout the
record, but the collection is marred by a persistent feeling that
Páez cannot duplicate the artistic success of *El amor*. Once
the album was released, both artists went public detailing how
unhappy they really were about the end result—and each
other. The friends became public, not intimate, enemies and
Páez returned a year later with *Abre* (Open), the strongest
record he had made in a long, long time.

Abre was produced by Phil Ramone, but the album initially
sounds like old news to anyone who is somewhat familiar
with the Páez aesthetic. The lyrics, however, are a different
story. Páez has always showcased a knack for impressionism,
filling his songs with vivid images of life in a third-world
metropolis. This time, he outdid himself with a veritable tor-

rent of metaphors and poetic musings that reveal the soul of a restless poet inside the body of a famous singer.

In "Al lado del camino" (On the Side of the Road) he recites a list of the events, people, and influences that made him the man he is today, spitting out the words like a machine gun.

> *Los libros, las canciones y los pianos*
> *El cine, las traiciones, los enigmas*
> *Mi padre, las cervezas, las pastillas, los misterios,*
>   *el whisky malo*
> *Los óleos, el amor, los escenarios*
> *El hambre, el frío, el crimen, el dinero y mis diez*
>   *tías*

> *The books, the songs, and the pianos*
> *The movies, the betrayals, the enigmas*
> *My father, the beer, the pills, the mysteries, the*
>   *cheap whisky*
> *The oil paintings, love, the stages*
> *The hunger, the cold, crime, money, and my ten*
>   *aunts*

It could be argued that in order to understand the music of Páez, you first need to understand the quirky idiosyncracy of his native Argentina. Petulant, nostalgic, viscerally emotional, and rigidly intellectual all at the same time, the Argentine is a walking contradiction, a melancholy European soul trapped in the body of a South American citizen.

Abre's centerpiece is the twelve-minute epic "La casa desaparecida" (The Disappeared House), a thorough description of the horrors and wonders of his country, which also applies to the realities of any post-dictatorship Latin American nation. "I've been traveling a lot lately, and everywhere I go, that song gets a very strong reaction from the public," Páez told me while in Los Angeles to promote the album. "I'm getting three-minute-long standing ovations after I perform it live. The kind of applause you see at an opera house, not within the setting of a pop concert."

The release of *Rey sol* (King Sun) in the year 2000, again with Ramone as producer, found Páez admitting openly in interviews with the Argentine press that, commercially speaking, things weren't what they used to be. He even ventured to say that people might have gotten tired of him. "*El amor* was a very high point for me," he said while visiting Los Angeles again to attend the Latin Grammy awards. "A very inspired record. It's very difficult to top that one."

But Páez pointed out to me that his best-selling effort was not necessarily the best one. "I know other people who prefer *Circo beat*," he told me. "Others say the last couple of albums I made are the best ones. It depends, really. I think my records are like a Pedro Almodóvar movie. When you buy one, you already have an idea of the kind of a vibe you are going to get."

An important part of this vibe is a melancholy that has permeated all of the singer's compositions since the beginning of his career. Even when he is celebrating the joys of romantic love, his melodies are tinged with nostalgia. "I'm basically a melancholy guy," he explained. "It's a fundamental element, not only to my music, but to all of Argentina's music."

It is not a coincidence, Páez pointed out, that the national music genre in Argentina is tango, the most lugubrious of dances. "We can't help it. It's part of what constitutes us as a nation. To deny that element is to deny our own history. This chronic melancholy is also translated, quite clearly, in our own aesthetic sense. The lyrical point of view. The way of phrasing."

Because of this ethnic characteristic, Páez told me that to him it was particularly important to learn how to get away from it. "The idea is to also stay away from it. And that's where new things, like a good sense of humor, come into place."

Even though the singer is extremely skillful at describing the intimate shadings of romantic love, his songs keep returning to the subject of his own country, a place that Páez refuses to leave. "My decision to remain in Argentina is a conscious and rational one," he added. "It's like, I'm staying in this *barrio* and I'm going to try to do everything I can for the *barrio*. I feel implicated here. I recognize the faces of the *pibes* (youngsters) and the old people. I want to leave my personal stamp."

Still, he is quick to emphasize that he is not in the business of saving anyone. Although he is the proud father of an adopted child and has, in the past, been involved with various charities, he said that he got into music in order to grow as a person. "I'm not in this for the money, and I'm not a singer only because I'm vain, although those two elements are an essential part of this business," he said with a self-deprecating smile. "The origin of it lies elsewhere. I'm in music for the freedom that it provides. I want some extra antennae in order to understand the world in a different way. If, in the process, I can make other people happy, that's even better."

Páez's last two albums to date are among his most uneven work. *Naturaleza sangre* (Nature Blood), released in 2003, sounds downright tired. *Mi vida con ellas* (My Life with Them), released in 2004, is a colorful, double-disc live collection culled from concerts recorded betwen 1994 and 2004 in Buenos Aires, Rio, Montevideo, Montreaux, Madrid, Bogotá, Guadalajara, New York, Los Angeles, and his native Rosario.

His live shows remain compelling. For a 2004 show at Los Angeles' Knitting Factory, he left aside the pop accoutrements of previous L.A. gigs and was backed solely by a near virtuoso trio of rock-solid guitar, bass, and drums—a move that added an extra level of urgency to hits such as "Giros" and the ever beautiful "11 y 6."

Páez's only weakness is a tendency toward the pedantic, what with his onanistic keyboard solos and a notorious antifan attitude that, in effect, does nothing but alienate him from his adoring crowd.

But he kept words to a minimum. Whereas the songs from *Naturaleza sangre* sounded just adequate, his classic fare from the eighties and early nineties has aged particularly well and deserves to be discovered by a wider audience.

A few years earlier, Páez had spent a good five minutes at the end of a Latin Grammy–related show asking the crowd to quiet down. He then launched into a haunting a capella (and mike-less) version of "Vengo a entregar mi corazón" (I Come to Offer You My Heart), his personal hymn of hope and redemption.

As he finished the tune, the ballroom was temporarily submerged in an unusual moment of complete silence.

"You see?" Páez said, a big grin on his face. "Not everything is lost."

Manu Chao

"EL MUNDO ES UN ASCO." Manu Chao spits out the words slowly and deliberately, a sad, defiant smile on his face. "The world is a disgusting place."

The statement comes out spontaneously on a lazy afternoon in 2001. We are in the empty patio of a West Hollywood café. The singer is talking about the state of the world, his nomadic lifestyle, and his new record.

Chao has the necessary life experience to support such a brutal statement. He has spent the better part of the last five years traveling around the globe, writing and recording music, his itinerary betraying a particular weakness for the most remote, inhospitable regions of the third world. "When you travel and see the poverty that most people live in, you are possessed by this overwhelming feeling of rage," he explains. "Then this internal struggle takes place, the moment when you decide to take that rage and channel it into something positive, like music."

That's exactly what the singer has done during a career that includes a stint as a founding member of the Franco-Hispanic collective Mano Negra and a solo career that produced *Clandestino*, a breakthrough solo album, and *Próxima estación: esperanza* (Next Station: Hope), his second album and the reason why Chao is sitting down with me on this particular afternoon.

If you're not familiar with Chao's subversive aesthetic, *Clandestino* is mandatory listening. You will discover a highly personal universe that sounds like the aural equivalent of a Federico Fellini movie, by way of Tijuana (one of his favorite places), Barcelona (the city where he lives), and the suburbs of Paris (the working-class environment where he grew up).

Chao's music is defined by a proliferation of sound effects (most of them culled from Latin radio stations), a collage of languages (he sings in English, French, and Spanish), and his ability to come up with sweet, ripe melodies that, upon further examination, reveal an underlying touch of regret. It is no coincidence that *Esperanza*'s closing tune is named "Infinite Sadness."

But Chao is much more than a recording artist. He has forged a reputation for dreaming up a series of highly improbable (and logistically nightmarish) projects—and then turning them into reality.

In the mid-nineties, Chao single-handedly resurrected an abandoned Colombian railroad track and toured the South American country, bringing a circus of sorts to every little village on his way. He remembers warmly that Colombia's bloody civil war would come to a brief halt wherever his train made a stop.

But a similar train trek through West Africa, a project that Chao hoped would materialize in 1999, was scrapped due to financial difficulties. "We couldn't find 'clean' money to do a tour like that," he says matter-of-factly. "We weren't really happy with the people who came forth to finance it. The French government also offered to contribute, but that's the dirtiest money in all of Africa," he adds, referring to the years of colonialism. "What France did to Africa is simply unspeakable."

Chao quickly replaced the train idea with a new vision: touring Europe with his new band, Radio Bemba, and using the proceeds from those shows to rent a couple of vans and do a series of gigs in various African countries.

"We can perform in the marketplaces," he enthuses. "Anywhere they let us play. We can just go there and play for free."

I ask Chao if his life as a wandering musician will ever come to an end. Would he ever consider settling down, maybe even marry his girlfriend?

"Right now, I feel very happy with her after two years of being together," he reflects. "But I don't really believe in the concept of marriage. It's a lie. Love is an adventure that continues every day. Today we're fine, we'll see about tomorrow, and in any case we'll have to struggle every day to make it work."

I point out that his parents have remained married after decades of being together.

"Yes, some people manage to do that," he sighs. "But I'm different. I need my freedom. If I'm in a relationship, I need to know that there's no contract binding us. If we got married, the couple would be in danger."

The son of exiled Spaniards who found refuge in France, Manu Chao played with various underground groups until the formation of Mano Negra in 1987. Walking a parallel path to Argentina's Fabulosos Cadillacs, the group became instrumental in the coming of age of *rock en español*.

Following in the footsteps of Chao's favorite band, the Clash, Mano Negra fused reggae with rock, punk, and Latin rhythms, complementing its stirring musical cocktail with intelligent lyrics that reflected a radical, socially alert political ideology.

Mano Negra's first album, *Patchanka*, came out in 1988. A year later, the group released *Puta's Fever*, a more mature effort that led to a bitterly disappointing tour opening for Iggy Pop. *King of Bongo*, released in 1991, was performed mostly in English and French, followed by 1992's live album *In the*

Hell of Pachinko. Mano Negra's final effort, the apocalyptic *Casa Babylon*, was released in 1994, after some of its members had already jumped ship. The record included "Santa Maradona," a tribute to Argentine soccer player Diego Maradona.

To this day, Chao insists that a Mano Negra reunion is out of the question. "I just don't see the point," he tells me emphatically. "Mano Negro was at its best in a live setting, and right now I'm very happy with Radio Bemba, my new band. We're still getting used to one another—we need another year or two to sound really strong. But reforming the group would seem like taking a step backwards to me.

"There's this other group that I used to have called Los Carayos. I'd love to reform *them*. And I'm still collaborating with my brother [former Mano Negra trumpet player] Antoine. He used to work as a DJ in a Latin radio station where he had the freedom to play whatever he wanted. But then the whole Ricky Martin deal happened and they started instructing him to play that kind of stuff—so he quit. Now he's into pirate radio. He has his own station and broadcasts from wherever he pleases.

"The other guys are also busy with other things. Tom [Darnal] formed [electronica collective] P18. When my regular percussionist canceled on me because his wife was having a baby, I called [former Mano Negra member] Garbancito and invited him to tour with us. But he was too busy with his own band."

Clandestino came out in 1998. Recorded all over the world in a portable studio and boasting a carnivalesque, let's-dance-until-the-end-of-the-world feel to it, the album became an international sensation, selling over two million units worldwide. In the late nineties, *Clandestino* was the record to listen to for hip, young professionals living in Western Europe and South America.

In the United States, the album touched a different demographic group. Here, it was *rock en español* fans who embraced *Clandestino* as a cult item, recognizing Chao as one of the genre's true visionaries.

Próxima estación: esperanza explores many of the same ideas introduced in *Clandestino*—namely, the creation of a more sophisticated version of Mano Negra. In fact, one of the songs in *Esperanza*, the Bob Marley–inspired "Mr. Bobby," begins with the exact same hook as "Bongo Bong," *Clandestino*'s hit single.

"I can't really talk of any marked differences between the two records," Chao says candidly. "I used the same techniques and the same people on both. Some of the same samples. Songs that were recorded on my portable eight-track, the product of my traveling here and there. So I think of *Esperanza* as the little sister of *Clandestino*. It's like a family of related albums. Both are populated by what I call 'my little dwarves,' the sounds and samples that are such a big part of my world.

"But we also added some brass on *Esperanza*," he pointed out. "To begin with, I wanted to make a more joyous record because my life changed and I'm in a different space right now. To me, the instruments that best represent the energy of pure joy are the brass. So we picked up the phone and called a trombonist and a trumpet player. We made an exception to our rule of recording everything spontaneously on an eight-track, and we actually held a proper recording session. It wasn't at a studio, but rather at a friend's home that has good acoustics. It was in Barcelona. The guys came and in only three days, they added brass to forty songs."

Hardcore Chao fans will understandably accuse him of copying himself. But they would be missing the point. So exciting is Chao's radical take on popular music, so refreshing and inspiring his mixture of styles and nonstop barrage of ideas, that you easily forgive him for making a second round through a path that he has already explored. Sure, the motifs are the same, but they are far from sounding tired.

To Chao, the key to understanding this album lies in its title . . . and especially the word *hope*. "The only people who really understand the concept of hope are those who live in the poorest places in the world," he says. "To them, hope is not an abstract concept. Hope is a plate of warm food, it's an everyday thing. And you can learn a lot from that."

Chao: *When I was young, I was really afraid of dying. I was sixteen or seventeen, I would think of death and I'd get this bizarre feeling, like vertigo. I'd be completely paralyzed. Now I have no fear of dying whatsoever. I think that I've had a good life. I'm very thankful. I can die tomorrow and I'd be absolutely fine with it. Everything that happens from now on is an added bonus.*

From all the people in my neighborhood, I was the lucky one. I was the one who won the lotto, if you wish. I've made a living out of my passion for music, which is an enormous privilege. I don't know why that happened to me. Luck is just luck. There's no explanation for it. There's no rational explanation behind it.

The other day I was reminiscing about my years in the bar-
rio with an old friend of mine. It was a working-class neigh-
borhood near Paris, where the old Renault factory used to be
before they closed it down.

I wasn't one of the dangerous ones. But the bad guys of
the gang always wanted me near when they robbed a gas sta-
tion or broke into an apartment. I was like a mascot for them.
They thought I brought them good luck. I was scared, but I
also had a morbid sort of curiosity and wanted to be there. I
didn't do anything but maybe drive a car, keep watch for
them—small things like that. But I led something of a double
life. I'd go to school during the day, and then I'd get to see
some pretty heavy stuff at night. Those guys taught me a lot
about the street. I don't know why, but they really liked me.
As a result, I was untouchable in the barrio. They never broke
into my parents' home.

When I go back to the neighborhood, I also feel lucky
because things haven't changed that much. The same old bar
is there. I still go to the back of the gas station to smoke a
joint. The only thing that has changed is that the guys are now
the children of the gang members I used to know. So I tell
them about the old times.

Chao's series of concerts to support the release of *Esperanza*
were highly uneven, revealing him as one of Latin rock's most
mercurial and unpredictable figures.

Performing at a Hollywood club, Chao spent most of the
evening revisiting the Mano Negra songbook. The result was
gripping and intense, but lacked the sophisticated textures and

emotional complexity of his solo work (most of Mano Negra's music sounded groundbreaking when released, but lost some of its edge with the appearance of the subsequent, more developed works of the many bands it inspired). When Chao tackled the new songs, he sped up the beats and simplified the arrangements, bringing them close to the furious Mano Negra aesthetic. The delicate nuances of the seductive "Bongo Bong," for instance, were sacrificed in the altar of the ever-moving mosh pit.

Chao clearly loved touring, and he continued to do so during the three years following the release of *Esperanza*, taking his sociopolitically alert musical circus everywhere from Chiapas and Quito to Sarajevo and Salamanca. The result was *Radio Bemba Sound System*, a twenty-nine-song, hour-long live album that puts you right in the midst of Chao's demented carnival.

Chao: *There's this policy that I follow once a tour has reached its end: I always split up the band and allow the musicians to rest and go back to their lives. After a month and a half, I call them up again. Are we up to playing more? Was the last tour so great that we want to do it again? The first person I ask these questions to is myself.*

Freedom is essential to me. My solo records have sold well, so there's always a certain amount of pressure from the label to go out and tour behind them. I guess my lifesaver of sorts is refusing to schedule anything for longer than six months. That's really important to me. I don't ever want to feel like I'm trapped in something resembling a career. The schedule can fill up quite fast, you know? All of a sudden, you have two years of your life written down on a piece of paper. That's dangerous. I'm not into that at all.

Then the fucking routine comes in and it's all downhill from there. I see lots of bands suffering from that. I don't think you play as passionately when it's your 128th show. There's something that gets lost on the way. Freshness is the most important element in Radio Bemba right now. And I feel that I have to preserve that. We can't lose it. I can't let that happen to the band.

Julieta Venegas

WHEN JULIETA VENEGAS released her much-anticipated third album in November 2003, her fans were understandably shocked.

Entitled *Sí* (Yes), the collection found the formerly introspective *chanteuse* from Tijuana singing about being happily in love, delivering her take on what a conventional pop record must sound like. Devoid of the singer's enigmatic lyrics, quirky instrumental flourishes, and unsettling textures, the record sounded strangely pedestrian.

Of course, anything by Venegas is at least marginally interesting, and *Sí* was no exception. Her unique vocals—part sensuous diva, part teenage goofball—sounded liberated and defiant when contrasted to the minimalist arrangements at hand. On "Lento" (Slow) and "A tu lado" (By Your Side), she succeeded in creating instantly hummable choruses—unaware that it is her oblique hooks that are truly memorable.

The album cover showed a blissful Venegas dressed in a bridal gown, standing in front of a pink backdrop. Inside the CD booklet, there was an effusive declaration of love to her manager Juan Pablo Ohanian, whom the singer was dating at the time.

If Venegas' intention was to expand her demographics, she was definitely doing something right. *Sí* became Latin music's most compelling success story of 2004, selling more copies than her two previous albums combined, garnering a number of awards and introducing her to the mainstream—both in Mexico and the Hispanic United States.

But Venegas is quick to point out that this drastic change of style came naturally to her. She insists, in fact, that it came from the heart.

"When the record came out, a lot of people were surprised because it has such a strong pop feel to it," she told me during a lengthy conversation, sitting outside the Hollywood hotel where she was staying while performing a handful of shows in the Los Angeles area. "True, I wanted to follow a more traditional song structure this time around. But I did it intuitively, which is how I always work. Then the album became successful and people started talking. I'm sure it would be a different story if it hadn't sold well."

Meeting Venegas is a memorable experience. At thirty-four, she has a tendency to reveal her inner thoughts with a minimal amount of mental editing. She speaks in short, breathless sentences, punctuated by her lilting Mexican accent and occasional bursts of nervous laughter. She is not beautiful in the conventional sense of the word, but her attitude evokes the elegance and vibrant personality of Frida Kahlo.

"I wish everyone would judge my album for what it is," she adds. "If they don't like it, that's OK. I'm sure there are people who don't identify with a smiling outlook on things. In that sense, there's certainly a difference from my previous work."

"*Sí* is not a pop record like the ones Thalía makes, but it's certainly lighter than anything Julieta has done before," Cecilia Bastida, Venegas' longtime friend and keyboard player, told me. "I applaud any changes that she brings into her music as long as she is being honest with herself. The new record may seem simpler to some listeners, but that's exactly what Julieta was after—simplifying the structures of her songs."

In concert, Venegas wears colorful clothes and even dances a little. But the coquettish attitude and sexy poses of her latest promotional photos are worlds apart from her beginnings as a solo artist, after she left punk-rock collective Tijuana No! (where she met Bastida) and moved to Mexico City in search of a solo career.

"I didn't go to the city with the hope of finding success there," she clarified. "Things happened almost as if by accident. I know that the moment I get bored with this place, I'll move somewhere else."

Born in Tijuana to a conservative family ("my father wanted me to get married and have a lot of kids"), Venegas enjoyed life on the border to the fullest, consuming music and films from both countries. She listened to both the Cure and syrupy Mexican pop, watched cartoons in English, and discovered the fleshy poetry of the Spanish language.

"I was always obsessed with the thought that there was nothing special about me," she recalls with the kind of disarming candor that sets her apart from so many other rock performers. "I don't have a great voice. I'm not a great pianist. I play the accordion, which is kind of weird. I spent most of my time locked inside my home writing songs. I needed someone from the outside world to validate my efforts. When a label signed me and bankrolled my first album, I just couldn't believe it."

Venegas' debut, 1997's quietly seductive *Aquí* (Here), introduced her as a serious artist, a talent to watch in the burgeoning *rock en español* field. It was produced by Gustavo Santaolalla, who was also at the helm of Venegas' masterpiece, 2000's *Bueninvento* (Goodinvention)—one of the most brilliant albums in the entire genre. American journalists dubbed her Mexico's PJ Harvey. "That's such a first-world way of describing me," she said laughing when I mentioned the comparison to her. "Nobody in Mexico has ever compared me to her."

A mesmerizing cornucopia of catchy hooks, bittersweet lyrics, old-fashioned accordion lines, and sloppy, homemade electronic effects, *Bueninvento* pulls you in and forces you to embrace its quirky, one-of-a-kind aesthetic. The record finds Venegas playing the accordion with the intensity of a norteño superstar, then distorting its sound until it becomes as thorny as a punk guitar. Although her melancholy face and the twisted urgency of her delivery reflect the open wounds of your typical rocker, this singer is a popster at heart, with a mischievous preference for loungy organ flourishes and bouncy drum machines. It's a delectable contradiction: At times, her open vowels overflow with a tragic sort of longing. Then again, her sugary hooks make you close your eyes and smile with contentment.

Venegas: *I definitely think of myself as a genuine* tijuanense. *Born and raised in Tijuana. My family still lives there, so I try to visit and play there as often as I can. Any excuse is good for that. And whenever I find myself there, I realize that Tijuana continues to inspire me in an aesthetic way. Perhaps it's because the city resonates with my childhood memories, but I think it's more than that. It's a weird location, Tijuana. There's no other place in the world like it.*

There were a number of situations during my childhood that marked me. We were four brothers and sisters and I had a hard time communicating with people as I was growing up. I was very insecure, I argued with everyone, and I felt perpetually misunderstood. There was a time when I even stopped talking to my twin sister, Yvonne.

Eventually I realized my place in life had to do with music. My parents made me take piano lessons, and I quickly noticed that I had a good ear for it. I would go to my class without studying and the teacher would still congratulate me for my efforts. It was a way of marking my own territory, establishing an identity: I'm the one who plays the piano, the music maker.

My parents didn't get along too well. My father was a bit of a tyrant. He wanted to control everything. When we were in our teens, he was the kind of dad who would let us go to one party a month. At 11 P.M. he'd be at the door waiting for us, and he'd go inside and look for us if we didn't come out. It's difficult to become a sociable young lady under those circumstances.

"You shouldn't study music," he'd say. "You should have a decent career and then get married." I'd tell him that I didn't want to waste his time or mine by studying something that I didn't like. "What are you are gonna do?" he'd ask me. "When your kids are at home and you go out every night to perform at the cabaret?"

I guess it's no wonder that I left Tijuana at twenty-one. I ran away. I couldn't live like that anymore.

Now my father has changed. He feels sorry for what he said in the past and his attitude is so passive that it's a little too much for me. I find it sad. Like many Mexican fathers of his generation, he has a hard time communicating what he feels.

The concert tour to promote *Bueninvento* created an indelible impression on me. Live, Venegas had no problems capturing her audience's attention. Her thin frame swaying subtly to the beat of her unusual melodies (they can switch from orgiastic funk to delicate lullaby in a nanosecond) she alternated between keyboards, accordion, and guitar, smiling shyly at the members of her band, looking lost in the dreamy textures of her own inventions. As a singer, Venegas breaks up syllables and accentuates vowels in unusual, yet bewitching new ways.

She shone on sophisticated ballads such as "Sería feliz" (I'd Be Happy), a tune inspired by the nostalgic style of sound-track composer Ennio Morricone.

The fact that she was able to project such an assured persona was even more impressive considering she had a number of obstacles to overcome: she was backed by a group that was only marginally equipped to translate her crafty songs into a tight live experience. Although it was a joy to watch Bastida on keyboards, the somewhat anemic rhythm section failed to match the urgency of the original studio versions.

Then again, instrumental prowess becomes less important with a voice of her caliber. A fittingly melodramatic version of the José José pop standard "El triste" (The Sad One) revealed Venegas at her most vulnerable.

There's a riveting darkness about Venegas' stage presence, the kind of sweetly disturbing eccentricity you are likely to find in a Tim Burton movie. Furthermore, the singer's lyrics of wounded idealism and wrecked love affairs inspire a direct association with a rich Mexican tradition of popular music imbued with bitter fatalism.

Listening to "Amores Perros" (a single based on a highly successful Mexican movie of the same title), it is easy to connect the dots between Venegas and the scores of venerated Mexican performers who have explored similar themes in their music, from Agustín Lara and Lola Beltrán to Juan Gabriel and José José.

Just like her fellow countrymen Café Tacvba (who lent her a hand producing part of *Bueninvento*), Venegas' hip sensibility has allowed her to modernize this tradition, successfully transposing it to the world of alternative rock.

"My theory is that it was during the *Bueninvento* tour that I became a more extroverted performer," Venegas explains. "It was such a complex record that I started acting out the songs in order to draw the audience in.

"Now people see it the other way around," she adds. "They tell me that I changed because I've released this pop album, but it's not like that at all. In fact, I was able to make this record because I changed first and grew up as a performer."

The story of *Sí* may sound like an overnight success. But for Venegas, the road to that album was slow and arduous.

Once the *Bueninvento* tour was over, she found herself writing yet another batch of songs about heartache and regret—a direction that she saw as a creative dead end. She sent a few demos to Santaolalla, but the producer refused to work with her a third time. It was then that Venegas thought of establishing a partnership with another songwriter. She flew to Madrid and met with Argentine singer/songwriter Coti Sorokin. They hit it off right away.

"The chemistry was just incredible," she says. "Coti would sit down with his guitar and, for a change, I would just be singing. We wrote a song a day—five of those tunes ended up on the album."

According to Venegas, it was Sorokin who pushed her to follow a more traditional songwriting recipe. She also studied the songs of the Beatles and Prince, looking to distance herself from the loopy experimentalism of her previous work. A wider audience followed soon.

In 2004, Venegas presented the new album during a sold-out show at the Conga Room in Los Angeles. "Something is changing," she sang during the opening number. "You may not see it/But I do feel/Something is changing inside me."

No kidding.

At the Conga, Venegas proved that, at the very least, the recent changes in her life have made her a happier person. Dancing rambunctiously across the stage and exalting the joys of romantic love whenever she spoke to her highly receptive audience, she infused the new material with an exuberant vocal energy that was hard to resist.

When it came time to perform the old *Bueninvento* and *Aquí* nuggets, they sounded liberated from the gloomy, nocturnal ambiance that used to be Venegas' domain. Old and new songs merged together in a combustible mix that brimmed with unexpected touches of old-school funk and R&B.

Venegas' quest for a fresher sound was helped by the raucous vibe of her four-piece band. Bastida's keyboard work was particularly illuminating. Her minimalist, yet evocative chords—along the lines of Brian Eno—added a welcome touch of mystery to Venegas' crystalline pop confections.

Venegas: *Whenever I'm invited to media parties, awards ceremonies, and glamorous events like that, I inevitably feel out of place. I get this bizarre sensation, like something is missing. I get nervous and stress out about my hair.*

I actually feel exactly the same way musically. I don't feel like I belong to this exclusive club of musicians and songwrit-

ers. I feel like that with a couple of friends, like Café Tacvba and Aterciopelados, but that's about it.

I've met a number of famous artists who have lost their sense of perception. They're out of touch with the outside world and talk to you only to hear themselves talk. They don't even listen to music anymore. Now that's serious. If you're a musician and you don't even listen to music, then you've really lost it.

Being nominated for a Latin Grammy is just fine with me. In fact, it's an additional weapon that I can use with the record company. "See? I've made my albums the way I wanted to, and it was because of that artistic freedom that I got a Grammy nomination." It gives you credibility, which is perfect for artists like me who don't sell a million records.

The question is not where my insecurity comes from. The question is how did I manage to find enough self confidence to continue doing what I do. I didn't wake up one day and say "I am an extraordinary singer and this is what I do." When I started writing songs, I just stayed at home. I was embarrassed. Then I started playing with Tijuana No!, but that was a different deal. We played ska and reggae. They were my friends. Even with them, I still felt like an oddball. "You dress like an old lady," they would tell me. "Your musical taste is so weird." I always felt like an outsider.

I had to go through the process of slowly learning to believe in myself, to believe in my capacity to express my feelings. It's been a complex process. Musically, believing that I can write and record my songs. Then, in a live setting, that I can perform in concert and communicate with my audience. It happened very slowly. But I'm not trying to sound humble

*here—it was slow because I'm a skeptic by nature, and all my
skepticism is usually directed at myself.*

In 2005, Venegas was invited to perform on the legendary television show *Sábado gigante*—the epitome of mainstream
accessibility as far as the Hispanic media is concerned.

"The other guests were a soap opera actor and a Miss Universe winner," she says. "And you know what? They were
really nice. As a rocker, I used to be prejudiced against people like that. But I've learned to take myself less seriously.
Now that I've been in the mainstream, I know that it's OK to
be there. It doesn't mean that you're a different person, you
know. You can still be yourself, no matter what."

Babasónicos

DESCRIBING THE MUSIC of Babasónicos is no easy task. The magic of what they do is elusive indeed. "Most people don't know what to make of them," a *rock en español* connoisseur I know told me. "Once they get it, though, they become addicted to their sound."

Critics have attempted to pin down the Babasónicos aesthetic into a specific formula of recognizable styles. You may be able to recognize a number of influences in what they do, but they sound like no one else, and each album they make is different from its predecessor.

Infame (Infamous), the group's 2004 masterpiece, may be somewhat easier to describe. Imagine a perfect cross between the sophisticated glam-rock of Roxy Music and the greasy Latin pop of crooners such as Sandro or José José. *Infame* takes the beauty of its own melodies seriously, yet it mocks everything around it with its savage wit. It is hot and cold, cryptic and accessible, sugary and bitter—all at the same time.

Babasónicos began as the ultimate cult group, years before they crossed over to the Latin American mainstream. The group was formed in Lanús, a neighborhood in the outskirts of Buenos Aires. The early albums are rough and unpredictable: 1992's *Pasto* (Grass) (an auspicious debut); 1996's *Dopádromo*; 1997's *Babasónica*.

In 1999, *Miami* was the first installment of an imaginary trilogy of sorts that found the group reaching its true potential. The album begins with "4 A.M.," a haunting, cinematic song about a girl who abandons her family and escapes with her boyfriend in search of adventure and romance. It is an Argentine version of the Beatles' "She's Leaving Home," performed by reclusive Babasónicos singer Adrián Dárgelos as a dark hallucination, complete with surf guitars, vigorous percussion, and lush washes of keyboards.

Jessico, released in 2002, began with an equally potent track. "Los calientes" (The Hot Ones) was hummable and poppy, marked by Dárgelos' flirty delivery:

> *Si no te apreciara tanto*
> *Te daría un beso que te haría temblar*
> *Como yo te aprecio mucho*
> *Te lo voy a dar igual*
>
> *If I didn't like you so much*
> *I'd give you a kiss that would make you shake*
> *Since I really do like you*
> *I'll kiss you just the same*

Jessico was named Album of the Year by the Argentine edition of *Rolling Stone* magazine. Latin rock insiders began to pay attention.

Two years later, *Infame* improved on its predecessors by surrendering to the guilty pleasures of vintage Latin pop, a decision that came naturally to Dárgelos.

"Before writing the songs that would become *Infame*, I realized that the world of mainstream rock had become a farce," Dárgelos told me. "On the one hand, you had the prefabricated, cliché-ridden corporate rock of Evanescence or Linkin Park. On the other hand, you had the retro-rock of the White Stripes or the Strokes, which was essentially all about the spirit of rock regurgitating itself. There was no exit."

Onstage, Dárgelos comes across like an extravagant combination of Mick Jagger, Freddie Mercury, and David Bowie.

A scrawny man blessed with the nasal voice of a neighborhood *bolero* singer, he will stop at nothing when it comes to entertaining an audience—wiggling his tongue provocatively, dancing spastically to the guitar solos, and emphasizing the more suggestive lyrics by staring into the audience with a perverse, if slightly dazed, look in his eyes.

But on the phone during a placid Buenos Aires afternoon in between tours, he sounds contemplative and shy, discussing the aesthetics of rock with the seriousness of a philosophy major.

"What was I to do? Become a retro-rocker?" he continues. "I felt that the only thing left for us to do that would embody the spirit of rock 'n' roll was to borrow elements from Latin American pop, a genre that is usually looked at with contempt."

From beginning to end, *Infame* offers an incisive meditation on the state of contemporary rock, but from a pop perspective. "Let's leave all criticism behind/Music has no message left to give," Dárgelos sings gleefully on the humorously titled "Scorpions Fan," a reference to the German hard-rock band. "Boys and girls dancing/At the funeral of rock 'n' roll," he chants on "Once," the closing track and the only moment in the album that borders on heavy metal.

But the collection's strongest asset is the sheer pop beauty of its melodies, from the rollicking energy of the opening "Irresponsables" (Irresponsible) and the wide-eyed sweetness of "Gratis" (Free) to the melodramatic pathos of "La Puntita" (The Little Tip), the one track on the album that sounds as if it had been recorded decades ago by a cheap Latin cabaret crooner.

"Artists like Sandro are more than just a *kitsch* influence to me," explains Dárgelos. "Those Latin pop sounds belong to my fantasy world as a musician because I absorbed them intuitively while I was growing up."

Dárgelos: *There are two kinds of artists: those who are thinking about making money and those who suffer because they are obsessed with an idea and are trying to get it out of their system. There are instances when having an idea in your head becomes too much—you just need to share it with others. That's what happened to me with* Infame.

The idea of having a revelation was my favorite theme throughout the making of this album. What's a revelation? It's an instance that makes you become conscious of a situation and changes your understanding of your surroundings. You will never be the same. This can happen on an everyday basis. We tend to think of an epiphany as something supreme that takes place toward the very end of a cycle. I don't see it that way. A life devoid of revelations must be horrible.

Whenever I listen to a song or experience the beauty of a stunning work of art, I am transformed. The process is not immediate. It evolves. In the beginning, I am moved by the experience. Then it grows on me. As the days go by, I understand the world in a slightly different way because my perception of this particular work of art has transformed me. This transformation became a revelation. Infame *works on those same principles. I believe music should embody just that: a search for revelation.*

Infame's most poignant moment arrives with "Putita," the record's fifth track. The title itself is something of a shocker:

"Little Whore." The contrast with the song's lilting guitar line and Dárgelos' straight-faced, melancholy delivery is simply delicious.

Ya sé, el camino a la fama no significa nada
Si no hay una misión
¿Cuál es?
Hacerte muy putita, probar tu galletita, con toda
*   devoción*

I know, the road to fame is meaningless
If devoid of a specific mission
Which one would that be?
To turn you into a little whore, to taste your little
*   cookie, with all my devotion*

The band's perverse sense of humor is patent. But the song sends you on a loop, disguised as it is in the shape of an achingly beautiful chorus.

Sos tan espectacular
Que no podés ser mía nada más
Tenés que ser de todos

You're so spectacular
That you can't just be mine
You have to belong to everyone

Is this the kind of rhetoric that all those gentlemanly *bolero* singers from yesteryear would have liked to use in their songs? To be able to call the object of their unrequited love a little whore? Does the song mark the liberation of the Latino love song in the new millennium? Musically, "Putita" is as gorgeous as "Bésame mucho" or "Piel canela." It has the smell of a classic, the instantly memorable lyrics—like slogans, they stay in your mind, a perfect combination with the nostalgic melody at hand.

"Putita" encapsulates the beauty of Latin rock. Its irreverence and total lack of formality combines with its appreciation for the old genres and potent properties of a timeless melody.

Dárgelos: *I don't really favor using irony in my songwriting. You know who I think the little whore in the song really is? It's me. What is the road to fame good for? Only to commit an aberration. I'm mocking myself for having arrived where I am. Now that I'm famous, everyone's expecting me to deliver a nice message. But I won't do that. In fact, I will try to generate the worst possible message, so that I won't become a cultural sort of chewing gum. I'm gonna give you a number like "Putita."*

There's a song by Tuxedo Moon called "In a Manner of Speaking." It talks about searching for the magic word that will open up all the doors leading to a woman's heart. The one word that is so concise, that it practically says it all without saying anything. "Putita" would be the antithesis of that.

At the same time, people in Argentina knew that I was recording a follow-up to Jessico, *which had been very successful. So they knew that the new album would be a hit, even if it was a piece of trash. Well, I wasn't about to deliver a pas-*

teurized product that could be easily consumed. No, I would create something that would be as contaminating and damaging as possible. Why? Because that's what I want. I seek chaos. Or at least, I want to confuse you with an ambiguous moral that will make you think twice about what's right and what's wrong.

Molotov

THERE ARE PEOPLE who think of Molotov as a fun, raucous act, blessed with a subversive sense of humor and plenty of *cojones.* Others regard the Mexico City quartet and its deafening sonic attack as the devil incarnate.

Both sides are probably right.

That said, there's no denying the exuberant personality of the band's 1997 debut *¿Dónde jugarán las niñas?* The desire to shock is evident in the wicked cover art—picturing a schoolgirl in a suggestive pose—and the album's title itself: "Where Will the Little Girls Play?" a pun on the best-selling *¿Dónde jugarán los niños?* (Where Will the Children Play?) by bland popsters Maná.

That collection's vitriolic wit and crass language shocked Mexico's conservative society, delighted its youth, and went on to sell 1.2 million copies worldwide—a staggering number for Latin rock.

Molotov combines rap with punk and hardcore. The band boasts two bass players (Paco Ayala and Mickey Huidobro), a singer/guitarist (Tito Fuentes), and American drummer Randy "Gringo Loco" Ebright. Molotov's lyrics are bilingual, relishing the opportunity for crass wordplay that only the combination of two different languages can provide.

Throughout the years, the foursome has incorporated other influences and refined its sound. Still, nothing beats Molotov's debut when it comes to sheer explosiveness and attitude.

Songs such as "Puto" (Faggot) or "Cerdo" (Pig) are sonically brutal, but unexpectedly sophisticated in the mixing of rap dynamics, pop punch, and hilarious lyrics. Masterfully conducted by producer Gustavo Santaolalla, this insane *rap en español* opera was initially banned from stores in Mexico

City. The controversy benefited the band and the single "Gimme the Power" became a huge hit.

During the first three decades of *rock en español*, the political oppression instituted in many Latin American countries forced artists to protest the state of the world with carefully crafted symbolism. Being blatantly critical meant either being banned and ostracized, or risking the chance of being kidnapped, tortured, and murdered. From the nineties on, musicians were able to say what they wanted to say, any way they wanted to say it.

Molotov's debut raised the stakes as far as how outspoken you could be about criticizing the establishment and still get away with it. Did this newly acquired freedom help the music, allowing it to liberate itself and explore new territories? Sure it did.

Molotov's superb "El carnal de las estrellas" (Friend of the Stars), the only new song in the band's 1998 remix collection *Molomix*, is one of the quartet's best efforts, picking up where *¿Dónde jugarán las niñas?* left off. Combining funky electric guitars with a full string section that gives the song a lush, filmic quality, "El carnal" finds Molotov unleashing a furious rap against the imperialistic, patronizing attitude of Mexican television.

"That song had more of a funk angle to it in its original incarnation," explained Mickey Huidobro, the song's composer, during a thoughtful interview that made me realize that Molotov's music was not only about bodily secretions and sophomoric jokes. "We added some minor chords that gave it a sinister touch. Gustavo [Santaolalla] suggested we add strings to it, and the final result ended up sounding really dark and macabre."

The song mentions specific names of companies (Televisa, Mexico's reigning television network) and presenters (Raúl Velazco, whose *Siempre en domingo* show was a television staple in that country for decades), before naming artists such as Luis Miguel, Mercurio, Paulina Rubio, and Magneto, which in Molotov's opinion are prefabricated and deplorable.

"'El carnal' talks about all the people who are abusing the medium of television in order to sell their plastic artists to the world," Huidobro said. "Televisa is nothing but a disgusting, cursed castle.

"These executives go to the streets and grab young ladies whose only talent lies in knowing how to smile, going to the gym, getting breast implants, and fucking the producers. Television has created this image of what people should look and sound like, which we think is terribly wrong. People should be able to look and be just the way they want to."

Anybody who's remotely familiar with the politics of television in Latin America knows that the exchange of sexual favors for a chance at stardom is routine business. "We think that the attitude of these producers is an insult to people's dignity," Huidobro added. "They'll even go after the men—there's nothing that gets in the way of satisfying their sexual needs. Plus, these acts are occupying precious television time that should be given instead to real musicians who spend their days living for rock 'n' roll, carrying their own instruments around and playing gigs without making a dime. Molotov is popular now, but before we formed the band, all of us spent years practicing our instruments and trying to make it, which is very hard over here."

After the release of *Molomix*, the unthinkable happened: one of the band's shows was attended by none other than

Paulina Rubio. "It was really funny, because at one point we announced that Paulina Rubio was in the audience and that we wanted to dedicate a song to her," recalls Huidobro. "It was 'El carnal,' of course. When the audience heard the chorus, they started to point in her direction in a humiliating way. You could see Paulina shrinking in her chair."

At the time, Huidobro understood that a lawsuit from Televisa was very much a possibility. "If they sue us, we'll just have to deal with the repercussions of that," he said with conviction in his voice. "For now, we're very happy being able to say what we want to say. We believe strongly in karma, and we think that any wrong that people do eventually returns to haunt them."

Huidobro: *As a band, we became popular relatively quickly. But I've been playing the bass for over ten years now. That means saving money to buy strings and an amplifier, taking good care of the equipment, trying to get gigs, and playing for free. All those things are very hard to do here in Mexico. It takes a long time. If you work hard enough, though, it does happen sooner than later. You've made the effort. That's all that matters in the end.*

We definitely sound better in concert than on record. It's just difficult to capture on a record something that sounds really different from the rest of the stuff that's out there. As it is, the image of us as a group is already difficult to describe—a photo won't really give you a good idea of what we're all about. Sonically speaking, it's even harder.

Our ambition is to continue making music for people to like or dislike. Once it's out there, the rest is up to them. We're glad to be able to travel around the world promoting the albums that we've made. That's the most important part about being successful. Everything else that comes with it is just details.

In 1999, Molotov released its second full-length album, *Apocalypshit.* A darkly hued record, it failed to add any elements of substance to the group's successful aesthetic. *Dance and Dense Denso*, released in 2002, was a different story. The album lacked the overall impact of *¿Dónde jugarán las niñas?*, but there was a welcome feeling of maturity to tracks such as the racially charged, cumbia-tinged "Frijolero" (Beaner) and the wonderfully funky "No me da mi Navidad"—a hilarious take on the egocentric complacency that inevitably follows rock stardom.

Two years later, Molotov indulged in the obligatory rock conceit of a cover album. The resulting collection, *Con todo respeto* (With All Due Respect), was appropriately disrespectful and altogether hilarious. It is debatable, of course, whether Mexico's venerable Afro-Caribbean orchestra Sonora Santanera would appreciate the band's treatment of its classic "La boa," complete with grungy guitars and a touch of profanity. Overall, Molotov's approach is surprisingly tame and melodic, approaching Euro-pop trash ("Rock Me Amadeus," "Da Da Da") with childish glee and in the process delivering the most tuneful album of their career.

In 2003, I watched Molotov perform in front of a surprisingly empty house at a club in Orange County. Devoid of the usual vociferous fans chanting expletives and joining a riotous mosh pit, the concert offered a clear view of the band's many strengths and weaknesses. On the plus side, the band's easily identifiable sound was impossible to resist. And just as the quartet's creepy guitar riffs and double bass cacophony brought the whole thing dangerously close to self-parody, Molotov saved the day with inventive rhymes that oscillated between absurd grotesquerie and incisive social commentary.

On the minus side, the group's antics did tend to grow a bit tiring after a while. No matter how you look at it, the obligatory "Puto" singalong fest (the audience responds with unequivocal enthusiasm whenever they are urged to chant "Puto" by the Molotov gang) brings to mind a Neanderthal's idea of punk-rock heaven.

Fortunately, the group's own fame has had no visible effect on its members' attitude. Ignoring the embarrassingly low turnout, the band delivered a hefty two-hour set and even invited a handful of female fans onstage for the recklessly sexual "Changuich a la chichona."

The resulting scene, however, was far from decadent. Like Molotov's own music, it was mischievous and good humored, openly silly, and even a little naive.

El Gran Silencio

LISTENING TO TONY HERNÁNDEZ talk wistfully about daily life in his native Monterrey, you realize that this is a man who is deeply in love with his *barrio*.

"We put some tables on the street and barbecue *carne asada*," he says with a smile. "We take the boom box out and play the Beatles or La Tropa Colombiana. My wife, my mother, my father, people from the neighborhood. We talk about life, about the state of Mexico. We question ourselves. We're like gypsies."

The *barrio* is an ever-present source of inspiration in the music of El Gran Silencio, the *rock en español* quintet with rap undertones that Hernández founded together with his brother Cano in 1993.

In fact, one of the most powerful songs in the band's best album, 2001's *Chúntaros radio poder*, is "El retorno de los chúntaros" (The Return of the *Chúntaros*)—a breathless, evocative rap describing the band members' return to the neighborhood after an extended tour. "Everybody was so proud of us when we came back from our first big tour," he recalls. "My wife got all pretty for me. My friends came to my door so that we could go play soccer in the street. The old ladies from the block came to say hello."

A creative tour de force, the thirty-five-track *Chúntaros radio poder* positioned El Gran Silencio as one of the key bands in the Latin rock field. Its lightness of spirit made the other bands in the movement look heavy handed, and even somewhat foolish by comparison.

The band's growth has been swift. *Chúntaros* is the quintet's sophomore effort. Entitled *Libres y locos* (Free and Crazy), the group's 1998 debut created an instant buzz within the Latin rock community because of the ease with which it combined the rap lexicon with a *ranchera* sensibility. "We might be crazy, but we're not stupid," the brothers rapped on the infectious title track.

The album's hit was the poetic "Dormir soñando" (To Sleep While Dreaming), which combined a classic Mexican *ranchera* vocal line with the tasty accordion licks of a Colombian *vallenato* and a dreamy rap with quirky observations on life, the ambivalent nature of reality, and the sheer beauty of being alive.

In concert, everybody agreed, the group sounded vital and refreshing. Unlike other *rap en español* acts, they actually performed their music live with real instruments. An early fan was producer Rick Rubin, who after attending a Los Angeles gig called them up and offered to produce their next album.

As it happened, however, Tony, Cano, and their bandmates ended up producing the record themselves. And this time around, the music defies description. *Chúntaro radio poder* transports you to a day in the life of an imaginary radio station, complete with an army of popular Monterrey DJs taking turns in presenting the songs. The rap element is not as heavy now. There's an emphasis on more traditional songs here, some of which betray the group's weakness for the grandiloquent rock of Led Zeppelin and Pink Floyd.

These foreign influences, however, are buried underneath a barrage of swinging Latin American rhythms, from the local *norteño* to Colombia's cumbia and *vallenato*, all of them performed seamlessly by Campa, the band's full-time accordionist. A tribute to the Virgin of Guadalupe, Cano's naive "Círculo de Amor" is one of the most heartfelt numbers in the band's repertoire.

The one track that demonstrates the extent of the band's creative growth is the moody "Canción para un O.G.T." It was written by Tony in response to the defection of El Silencio's former bass player, who ended up suing the group. "This guy alleges that he made five thousand pesos a day with us when we were still playing shows for free, performing with these cheap rhythm machines," says Hernández. "I decided to write a song about him, but not in an aggressive mode. I would be just like him if I started to yell a barrage of insults. I chose to make it more of a personal song.

"I realized that the fault wasn't his alone. We had made a mistake, too. The group had been wrong in accepting him into the fold just because he knew how to play the bass really well. I wrote about the fact that you can't lie to yourself. The truth always surfaces in the end. When you go to bed at night and start looking back at the events of the day, you can't escape the fact that you have lied about something."

Musically, the song is richly layered. At times, it sounds like the kind of tune that Cornelio Reyna y sus Bravos del Norte could perform. But the actual sonics evoke the atmosphere of a trippy Pink Floyd workout.

"I see that song as a progressive *huapango* with touches of *norteño* and ambient," laughs Hernández. "It's in a minor key, so it's very atmospheric. I grabbed a turntable and recorded some scratches for it. Then I added some extra moods by lifting off guitars and strings from a couple of records. We also distorted the accordion. The tune functions in many different levels. It could be a small waltz or a rock sonata. A bellicose song that happens to be very sentimental at the same time."

Latin folklore has been a steady presence in *rock en español* since the nineties, but many of these purported homages were done tongue in cheek. You were never sure if Café Tacvba or Aterciopelados were paying respect to the music of their parents, mocking it, or doing a little bit of both. El Gran Silencio, on the other hand, can't hide its heartfelt admiration for the rural music of both Mexico and Colombia.

"When Tacvba released 'Ingrata' in 1994, I really felt that they were mocking the *norteño* people and the music from the *cantinas*," agrees Hernández. "And most of the *rockeros* I encounter think that cumbia is an artless form. But that's not true. Some of the best bass players I've listened to lately come from cumbia and *vallenato*."

These Colombian genres are especially popular within Monterrey's working class. Their fans are sometimes called *chúntaros*, a derogatory term that the band has made its own by altering its meaning. Within the Gran Silencio aesthetic, a *chúntaro* is someone who is honest with himself, enjoys freely his own quirky taste for things, and doesn't care what other people think of him.

Not surprisingly, Hernández explains, the one band that El Gran Silencio identifies the most with is *norteño* superstars Los Tigres del Norte. Just like Los Tigres, El Silencio has the satisfaction of its fans as a number-one priority. And they do everything in their power to avoid the trappings of fame.

"If I pretended to be a rock star and spent my nights partying at discos after the shows, right now I'd be writing songs about *estupideces* (stupid things)," he says candidly. "That's why I'd rather come back home and spend time with my family. I watch a bit of television, listen to my favorite DJs on the radio, and record bootleg CDs of rare Colombian music for my friends in the neighborhood."

Popularity has its price.

El Gran Silencio's third album, 2003's *Super riddim internacional, vol. 1*, began with a hilarious collage of street interviews in which a number of people are dissing El Silencio in every conceivable way.

At first, the album appears to be all about the sweet cumbias and chant-along rhymes one has come to expect from such a party-friendly band. But there's plenty of reflection beneath the festive atmosphere. "El espejo" (The Mirror) finds Tony pondering the benefits of maturity, whereas "Sueño" (Dream) is an arena-rock lament done in blood-dripping *ranchera* style. By the time you reach the effusive outro of snippets from fans praising the group for its inventiveness, you realize that El Silencio is one of those rare Latin bands that make you think and dance at the same time.

El Silencio's overzealous critics have complained about the Hernández brothers' lack of focus when it comes to the art of songwriting. Their coarse blend of *ragamuffin* and Colombian vallenato, they say, becomes childishly repetitive after a couple of tunes. And that their instrumental ability is merely enough to get by.

And yet, El Gran Silencio offers one of the most joyous and compelling live shows in Latin music. I saw them live a number of times in 2003 and 2004, and was always inspired by El Silencio's ability to celebrate everything that is worth celebrating about Latin rock.

At a sold-out show at Los Angeles' House of Blues, Tony and Cano emphasized the kind of bare-it-all emotional openness that is consistently present in quality Mexican music, regardless of genre. The focus was on the audience at all times—creating an instant rapport that suggested a communal carnival more than a conventional concert.

Beginning with a trilogy of rollicking numbers ("Sound system municipal," "Cumbia lunera," and "El retorno de los chúntaros"), El Silencio launched an unstoppable sonic attack that more than made up for the loose structure of their songs.

Boosted to a ten-piece unit, the band was wise to incorporate the basic configuration of an Afro-Caribbean orchestra, with a brass (saxophone, trumpet, trombone) and percussion section (congas, timbales, trap drums).

El Silencio's aesthetic may be defined by its reckless enthusiasm, but the band is wise to keep its shows short and sweet—their concerts feel like a pleasant dream that ends a few moments too soon and leaves you pining for more.

Orishas

RAPPING IN SPANISH is no walk in the park. A quintessentially American art form, rap tends to suffer in the hands of Latino MCs who attempt to transpose its elusive aesthetic into Spanish. The results usually fall somewhere between the monotonous and the downright pathetic.

During the nineties, groups such as Control Machete, Los Tetas, and Illya Kuryaki and the Valderramas gained popularity attempting to transpose the hip-hop aesthetic into the Spanish vernacular. It was a difficult task. Except for El Gran Silencio, none of these groups managed to create a distinct musical statement because of the lack of a unifying concept.

A collective of Cuban expatriates based in France, Orishas finally found one.

Its four members rap, sure, but deep inside they're still *salseros* with a serious weakness for the sinuous spice of *son montuno* piano lines, the comforting darkness of Yoruba religion, and the snappy rhymes to be found within the labyrinth of the Castilian language.

"We have destroyed a lot of preconceived ideas of what Latin music is supposed to sound like," admitted Yotuel "Guerrero" [Warrior] Manzanares, one of the group's rappers, during an interview conducted in 2000. "We've combined hip-hop with the most sublime, authentic elements of Cuban *son*, *timba*, and funk."

Originally, rappers Yotuel and Ruzzo were members of the Cuban hip-hop group Amenaza. While in Paris, the two hooked up with MC Livan Alemán and the melodious voice of singer Roldán Rivero, who then belonged to a local group of traditional Cuban music.

The resulting quartet recorded *A lo cubano* (Cuban Style) with notable French hip-hop producer Niko Noki—the architect of Orishas' sensuous sonics. Instead of relying on the genre's traditional loops and samples, they created richly layered backing tracks using piano and harpsichord, trumpets and trombones, the tasty sounds of the Cuban *tres*, as well as a string ensemble.

But the most important guest musician was Angá Díaz, a ferocious conga player and one of the most gifted percussionists to come out of Cuba in the last decade. Angá was responsible for some of the tasty polyrhythms on top of which the four Orishas engage in their trademark verbal acrobatics.

Lyrically, *A lo cubano* covers a variety of themes. On "Represent," the rappers express a sweet longing for their homeland. "Madre" is a love letter to their mothers. The title track showcases the collective's goofy humor, with a bit of Chinese rapping thrown in for some politically incorrect fun. And the bouncy "Atrevido" is a cautionary tale about the men who prostitute their women to the tourists who visit Cuba looking for cheap sex.

"We might be very poor, but we still know how to read and write," said Yotuel. "The fact that we live in a third-world country doesn't mean that we're out of touch with reality."

If there is one underlying theme that defines *A lo cubano*, that would be a relentlessly positive message in both music and lyrics.

"The Cuban ghetto might be different from the American ghetto, but it's still the same shit," emphasized Yotuel. "If you've made mistakes in your life, you have to do your best so that the following generations won't do the same things you did."

Which is why Yotuel is perplexed by the aggressiveness in some of the rap coming from the United States. "I don't understand," he commented. "They talk about inciting violence, killing your friends, treating women like whores. It's bizarre. In America, there's black rappers shooting one another, while some white guys are wearing Malcolm X caps."

Yotuel thinks that the power of hip-hop to communicate a message cannot be underestimated. "Rap is like a school where your fans listen to the stories you have to tell," he said. "That's why I don't like gangsta rap. If that's what rap is all about, then I'm not a rapper. I make a different kind of music."

Capturing the sophisticated textures of *A lo cubano* in a live setting was definitely a daunting task, but the group had no problem creating an electrifying show during a Los Angeles performance to promote the U.S. release of the album.

Beginning with a prerecorded sonic collage of Cuban oldies that paid respect to past masters such as Orquesta Aragón and Los Van Van, the three Orishas (rapper Flaco-Pro had left the group a few months earlier) were received like gods by the capacity audience. Their energy onstage was infectious and the sheer swing of their rhymes came to life that evening, evoking an aura of playfulness and bonhomie.

The trio was accompanied by an adequate percussionist and a DJ who experienced a number of technical problems during the concert. His vinyls had too many scratches on them, and the Orishas' acrobatic jumps on the wooden stage kept causing the turntable's needle to skip. The trio struggled to keep their rhymes on time, and the spotlight stayed firmly planted on the good-natured bravado that fuels their funky jams.

Two years later, the members of Orishas emerged as three wide-eyed idealists on *Emigrante* (Immigrant), their excellent second album. The beats (again, courtesy of Niko Noki) were supple and smooth, the melodies instantly hummable, and the trio's rhymes had an emotional transparency about them that set them apart from the competition.

On *Emigrante*, Orishas rap wistfully about their wives, their children, their bitter experiences as Latin American immigrants in a cold, European land. "We felt that the hip-hop market was saturated with aggressiveness, both lyrically and musically," said Roldán González, the group's *sonero*, during a telephone conversation from Paris. "A lot of gold chains and plenty of bad boys calling their women whores. That's definitely not our style. We also wanted to make an album that was more melodic than the first one."

Indeed, *Emigrante* has a depth and a sweetness to it that transcends the more gimmicky aspects of *A lo cubano*, while remaining quintessentially Latin. The video for the first single, opening track "¿Qué pasa?" (What's Up?), used evocative special effects in order to depict the trio as giants, roaming the streets of a dilapidated Havana. Other tunes were equally inventive. "Mujer" is a tender ode to womanhood. "Así fue" (That's How It Was) is a dark narrative about a love affair that benefits from the vocal interplay between the three Orishas. And "300 kilos" gave the ultimate proof of street cred for Orishas as valid members of the Afro-Caribbean family: Colombian *salsero* Yuri Buenaventura contributed his ragged *soneos* to the track.

Orishas returned in 2005 with *El kilo,* a smooth album that emphasizes smoldering vocal harmonies over the trio's trademark rapping. It was produced by Andrés Levín with intriguing touches of *boogaloo* but not enough fire to reach the level of vitality displayed on the group's previous two albums.

La Mala Rodríguez

THE VOICE ON the other end of the phone line is beginning to
sound tense and edgy. Even though the voice already has a
rough quality to it, with its flamenco tinge and brusque Sevilian accent, there's a layer of anger in it that's new and intim-
idating. There's no doubt about it: twenty-three-year-old
Spanish rapper "La Mala" (The Mean One) Rodríguez is losing her patience with me.

"So what are you saying?" she snaps after I mention the
myriad of heroin references to be found in her profanity-laced
rhymes. "Are you asking me if I do drugs? Sure, I've done
drugs. Big deal." Then, with the streetwise flow of a consum-
mate MC, she adds:

> *El que no fuma, ha fumado o va a fumar*
>
> *Whoever's not smoking, has already smoked or
> will soon be doing it.*

Welcome to the world of María Rodríguez Garrido, aka
Mala Rodríguez, the most explosive, enigmatic, and talented
rapper in the Latin world, regardless of country or gender. A
woman whose 2002 debut album, *Lujo ibérico* (Iberian Luxury), is the first recording that actually managed to cross over
to the rest of the world from Spain. Rap had been blossoming as an underground genre there since 1994, with notable
collectives such as Solo Los Solo, 7 Notas 7 Colores, and Vio-
ladores del Verso.

Unlike eclectic-minded rappers like Orishas or Vico C,
Rodríguez avoids a liberal fusion of genres. Furthermore, she
doesn't attempt to translate the aesthetic of rap, but rather

transposes it to the vernacular of Sevilla's barrios, while adapting it to her self-made persona as a callous, occasionally vicious, and always upfront independent woman with nothing to fear. What she's taken from her favorite MCs such as Snoop Dogg and Nas—the endless braggadocio, the concept of the opposite sex as a mere object of pleasure, the idea of an individual code of ethics that functions from within a marginalized world—she's tailored to the richness of the Spanish language and the ease with which it lends itself to humor and irony.

On "Tambalea" (Stagger), a number about Rodríguez's constant switching between being in and out of control, she displays a remarkable poetic imagination, spitting out an endless amount of rhymes ending with the "ea" sound (*jalea, marea, pelea, menea,* and an expletive or two to boot). The track is intensely sensuous and hypnotic.

On a videotaped interview that the U.S. branch of Universal Latino reportedly cajoled her into doing, Rodríguez looks like an ordinary teenager, a volatile combination of timid and rebellious. Her decision not to reveal her face on the album's art (the cover depicts her covered in shadows) or to shoot music videos to promote the project has done nothing but enhance her mystique.

During our thirty-minute phone conversation, the rapper is equally cryptic, whether conversing about her absent father ("I don't know who he is, and I don't want to talk about it") or her next album ("It'll be really big"). She sneers when I point out to her that her rhymes are devoid of any references to romantic love. *A mí me gusta la acción,* she says. "I love action—doing things, as opposed to talking about them."

Musically, *Lujo ibérico* has more than its share of uneven moments. At times, the production—courtesy of Jota Mayúscula and Supernafamacho, former members of the seminal Spanish rap collective El Club de los Poetas Violentos—fails to match Rodríguez's brooding delivery. That said, few *rap en español* albums deliver such an indelible artistic statement as *Lujo* does.

La Mala's flamenco tinge came naturally in her rapping, but some accuse her of using her Sevilian accent as a commercial gimmick. In any case, by the time she followed up a disappointing collection of b-sides and unreleased recordings (2003's *La niña/amor y respeto*—The Girl/Love and Respect) with her second full-length album (2004's *Alevosía*—Perfidy) she had already realized that the flamenco touch sold well and even ventured into a little bit of singing. This may explain why *Alevosía* feels at times like a lighter version of La Mala's style, even though her street cred is boosted with guest spots by rappers such as Kultama, Kamikaze, Supernafamacho, and Nut Rageous.

The change is evident from the slick-looking cover image—which depicts a defiant Mala dressed in a daring black dress that reveals her stomach and part of her breasts—to the opening track. Entitled "Lo fácil cae ligero" (The Easy Falls Down Quickly), this smooth exercise in pop combines La Mala's low-key delivery with mellifluous female vocals. *Alevosía* was not as powerful as *Lujo*, but it found La Mala embracing the commercial potential of her work without compromising her artistic ambitions. The video for the song "La niña" (The Girl) caused some controversy with its candid look at the life of a little girl who sells drugs as a means to get out of poverty—and the disturbing images of a gang shootout and a woman bleeding from the nose after snorting cocaine.

La Mala's first American tour had been nothing short of a disaster. She had performed at a New York club as part of the Latin Alternative Music Conference festivities in 2002. The venue was inadequate and some of her friends were allegedly not allowed in. The rapper was angry and had no desire to perform. Witnesses recall an uneventful performance by an artist who sounded much better on record than in a live setting.

A second tour took place in 2004, and La Mala's performance at the dingy Echo club in Los Angeles had more than its share of troubles. The concert was poorly attended, suffered from appalling sound, and was cut short by the venue before La Mala could deliver her biggest hit—"Tengo un trato" (I Got a Deal), *Lujo ibérico*'s opening track.

This time, however, La Mala did everything in her power to avoid repeating the New York fiasco. Dressed in tight jeans and an Adidas tank top, her expressionless face locked in a grimace of stubborn defiance and cool contempt, she began the show with a stunning *a capella* segment that showcased her ease for playing with the sounds of the Spanish language.

Her rhymes—apocalyptic tales of life in the Sevilla barrios—were intriguing enough. But it is in La Mala's seductive flow that Spanish rap has gained its most fiercely original MC.

Breaking up words, emphasizing unexpected syllables, she generated moments of raw poetry that had a brutal kind of beauty to them. Backed by MC Kultama and DJ Jotamayúscula, she explored a variety of moods, from the sinuous menace of "Tambalea" to the sensuous minimalism of "Lo fácil cae ligero."

Keeping the mannerisms of American rap to a minimum, she proved that *rap en español* has a seductive identity of its very own. After the show she stayed at the venue greeting her fans with undivided attention, snapping at the label's publicist whenever she tried to interrupt the short conversations she had with them.

Los Amigos
Invisibles

I'M LYING DOWN on the cold hardwood floor of a San Francisco recording studio. The year is 1999. The music that's being performed around me by six Venezuelan musicians is soft and soothing and exotic—everything that lounge music is supposed to be. I'm slowly falling asleep with a smile on my face.

I'm hoping that Los Amigos Invisibles will understand that I'm falling asleep not out of disrespect, but rather out of sheer contentment. The South American band has invited me to witness the recording of its third album, *Arepa 3000—A Venezuelan Journey into Space*. I'm even allowed to enter the actual recording space, as long as I lie down on the floor, a few steps away from the musicians, and don't make any noise.

The drummer is having a hard time getting a tricky time signature right, and the band is forced to play the same section of a tune dozens of times. All the better for me: I have no problem dozing off to this exquisite morsel being played over and over again on this sunny afternoon. For anyone who enjoys the melodious strains of Henry Mancini, Burt Bacharach, or Ennio Morricone with a simpatico dash of Latin cadences thrown in for good measure, Los Amigos are pure heaven.

In 1998, David Byrne's Luaka Bop released the group's second disc, *The New Sound of the Venezuelan Gozadera*, and Latin rock found one of its brightest hopes. On first listen, the sextet revealed itself as a tribe of musical scavengers, combining juicy bits of disco and funk with old-fashioned rhythms like the *cha cha cha* and the *bossa nova*. Los Amigos' sound was campy and retro, but the subtle influence of electronica gave their music a sophisticated, ultra-cool allure.

It may be tempting to categorize Los Amigos as a harmless diversion in *rock en español*, but doing so would be a serious misjudgment. The band is responsible for some of the most gorgeous musical moments in the entire genre.

Underneath party jams like "Cachete a cachete" (Cheek to Cheek) and "Ultra-Funk" lies the mature craftsmanship of guitarist José Luis Pardo. The group's main composer, he combines an instinctive understanding of vintage genres with an experimental vein that pushes him toward edgier sonic textures.

Growing up in Caracas during the seventies, Pardo would listen to the old-fashioned mambo and *bossa* tapes that his parents would play on a portable cassette player during the family's holiday trips. He remembers those early musical memories vividly. "Pérez Prado was the law in my house," he says. "I remember thinking that the mambo required a lot of musicians in order to sound good. The arrangements were so elaborate. The *bossa nova*, on the other hand, sounded elegant and naive, but also very complex."

Soon after the release of *Gozadera*, Los Amigos became critical darlings in Europe and the United States, and Madonna considered having them open for her on a world tour that never materialized. The expectation for the band's first new material in two years is tremendous, which is why I have taken an entire day off just to fly to San Francisco and see them record.

Los Amigos' manager Alberto Cabello and I gather at the mixing room and listen to early drafts of songs like "El sobón," about a guy who gets drunk at parties and paws the young ladies around him, and "Mami te extraño," a tropical blues lament about missing your beloved one.

There's also a scorching *bossa* tune that mixes the detached languor of lounge with the permanent sense of longing that defines the Latin American experience. "This is one of your tunes," I point out to Pardo, and he is surprised that I recognized his signature style, a subtle mixture of the old and the new.

Pardo's masterpiece is still the ethereal "Las licras del Avila," an instrumental *bossa* that begins with the sound of the needle touching a scratchy LP (one of producer Andrés Levín's gimmicks) and develops into a soulful composition that could have very well been written by Antonio Carlos Jobim. "Las licras" illustrates the wonderful paradox that is at the heart of Los Amigos Invisibles: this is music that is fluffy and soulful at the same time, superficial and profound.

Later on, I chat with percussionist Mauricio Arcas about rhythmic patterns on the *timbales*. In concert, Arcas shines performing a hilarious rap with the deadpan expression of a weary mafioso during the frisky Amigos favorite entitled "Ponerte en cuatro" (Put You on All Four), a paean to the joys of making love in a particularly scintillating position. Like the rest of the group, Mauricio has a friendly, casual attitude, as if he were still playing in a Caracas garage with his high school buddies.

The group's most enviable strength is its ability to write openly sexual lyrics with playful sincerity. This is probably the only band on the entire planet who can sing about the joys of anal sex ("El disco anal," complete with poppy chorus and a perversely happy keyboard line) and have the female audiences cheer approvingly.

Since some members of Los Amigos are married, I ask them about their wives' opinion on the sexually explicit nature of their lyrics. "They laugh," says Pardo. "We were already writing these kinds of lyrics when they met us. Our wives love the band because they see all the work that we have put into it. I guess it's their mothers who have reasons to worry."

I suggest to them that Los Amigos espouse a blissful state of perpetual adolescence. "We strive to be a band that makes you move your feet and dance," says Julio Briceño. "That has nothing to do with adolescence. Look at Venezuela's salsa singer Oscar D'León—he's around sixty and will have you up and dancing even if you're deaf. Youth is a state of mind." The band has been away from Venezuela for over two months now, recording and playing a few dates all over California. "I've known these guys all my life," bassist José Rafael Torres tells me a few minutes before I leave the studio to fly back home. "Being part of a band is like being married to five different people at the same time. Right now, we're living in a small apartment, all six of us sharing one tiny bathroom. . . ." He smiles at the insanity and coziness of it all, then sighs. "We've been very lucky. I can't think of anything else I'd rather do than be here with *mis amigos*."

In 1976, Venezuela decided to nationalize its oil industry and the country experienced an economic boom. This prosperity resulted in a number of unexpected developments, including a proliferation of tacky, expensive nightclubs. By the mid-eighties, though, Caracas was back to the usual Latin American standards of poverty and underdevelopment and most of the discos closed their doors. The decaying buildings sat there, abandoned but not forgotten, a silent reminder of the decadence that was and would never be again.

When echoes of the first raves reached the shores of Venezuela, the scene began to change. "You didn't need an abandoned disco anymore to have a party," Pardo told me a few years after the *Arepa* sessions during a telephone conversation from his home in Caracas. "A warehouse, a factory, any big building was good enough for a rave. There were no bathrooms and no alcohol. The only purpose of those gatherings was to listen to the music and take ecstasy."

But in the early nineties, just as electronica was taking the planet by storm, a few young entrepreneurs started to rent some of these run-down, empty discos and hold exclusive parties in them. A movement was born, relying on a new, imported subculture of DJs, techno beats, house, and acid jazz. According to those who were there to partake in the fun, the clandestine aspect of the whole thing gave these barely announced meetings a delicious feel.

"Los Amigos were the humble but brilliant pioneers of a movement that was based around the simple concept of uniting young people with similar interests and forming a real music scene," Alberto Wallis, a veteran club promoter from Caracas, told me.

The beginning of the end for the Venezuelan underground scene came in 1998. The party that ruined it all was held on a beach by the name of Patanemo. "It was a huge rave attended by people from all over the world, designed to coincide with a solar eclipse," recalled Pardo. "When the police raided it, they found everyone drugged out of their minds, dancing naked on the beach."

It was then that the authorities realized the amount of drug consumption that took place during these happenings. After that point, the raves were controlled severely and their audience shrank.

Still, Pardo, who continues to DJ to this day, said that the scene will always remain a cult phenomenon. "Most of the people who get involved in this are middle- to upper-class kids who want to imitate life in England or the United States. The movement will never go beyond the underground. Our country is not ready for it. This is Latin America. We live in a different reality here."

Arepa was a transitional album for Los Amigos. There was a great vibe to the sessions, but the songs lacked the focus of *Gozadera*. Los Amigos had tried too hard to make a commercial disc, and instead they were beginning to sound a little tired. Touring ceaselessly throughout the United States didn't help either.

The band's real crisis began in the fall of 2001, when it participated against its better judgment in the Watcha Tour Latin rock festival. Taking the stage at the Universal Amphitheatre during the trek's Los Angeles stop, the guys looked frail and exhausted as they performed a colorless half-hour set that was booed loudly by the event's hardcore rock fans. Just before departing the show's rotating stage, the usually even-keeled Briceño gave the finger to the crowd, his lips locked tightly in a grimace that expressed his anger and frustration.

"It was the lowest point imaginable," admitted Pardo during a 2003 interview. "It was pathetic, because we didn't want to be on that tour from the very beginning, but somehow we ended up doing it. And we lived through it. If you survive playing in front of fifteen hundred people who are throwing bottles at you and calling you *culero* (faggot), you can survive anything."

As it turns out, the Watcha fracas was the beginning of an extended, painful cycle that saw Los Amigos move to New

York City from their native Caracas, fire longtime manager Cabello (the man responsible for the Watcha booking), and hold up the release of their fourth album due to the financial problems of Luaka Bop.

"I don't really remember us discussing a possible break-up," said Pardo. "But we were all very dispersed, caught up in the midst of this bad momentum."

Then, unexpectedly, good things started to happen. Los Amigos' psychedelic soundscapes attracted the interest of artists outside the Latin rock circuit. Production team Masters at Work ("Little" Louie Vega and Kenny "Dope" González) suggested a collaboration, an offer the group was happy to accept. The Amigos were also delighted to hear from hip French DJ Dimitri from Paris, and ended up exchanging tracks for their respective albums.

"Working with DJs has changed our way of making music," offered Pardo. "These guys don't labor over what kind of pedal you should use with your guitar. They think in terms of the overall ambiance, the texture of the song. They leave all messages aside and strive to make music that envelops you."

One listen to a rough mix of the new album, which was eventually released as an import and came out in the United States in 2004, suggested a universe of changes. The songs were longer, profoundly nostalgic, imbued in the dreamy, sophisticated textures of ambient electronica.

"From the eighties on, everything started to sound over-produced," the guitarist told me. "The drums were too perfect. You discovered MIDI files and you lost your soul. The old LPs have mistakes in them, and there's something positive to be said about imperfection. Our music is an answer to all those issues."

❧

The stage was set for the release of Los Amigos' finest album, *The Venezuelan Zinga Son Vol. 1*. "I feel like we've been born again," enthused Pardo after the album release, adding that he was extremely proud of his new work with the band. "We're experiencing a new honeymoon of sorts. And we know that when the record is finally released this year, many people in the dance genre will be waiting for it."

Singer Briceño was equally enthusiastic. "A few months after recording *Arepa 3000*, we realized that it was too much of a pop record," he told me. "Maybe we were a little drunk on the success of *Gozadera*. The new album is less conventional—it has a psychedelic sound to it. I let the guys do their thing and saw my voice as another instrument in the band. I love the progression of the album from a soft, almost whispered beginning to a frantic finale of nonstop funk. We designed it the way you would plan a DJ set. Starting out with some chill-out stuff, then climbing in intensity, and bringing on the salsa tunes. I feel like we finally vindicated ourselves."

Zinga Son begins with "Comodón Johnson," a sprawling *bossa* with wordless vocals that evokes the placid mood of a summer afternoon somewhere in South America. The track is soaked in ambient sounds that enhance its dreamy mood. Birds chirp. A dog is heard barking in the distance. The result sounds strangely low-key at first—that is until you surrender to the languid pace and absorb the song's poignant emotionality.

Pardo, whose record collection includes as many as seventy different versions of "Girl from Ipanema," played three different tracks to his bandmates in an attempt to explain to them the kind of sonics that he had in mind for the recording of "Comodón Johnson": Michel Legrand's infamous theme for the sixties movie *A Man and a Woman*; a song by Stereolab; and an obscure piece by Italian soundtrack composer Ennio Morricone entitled "One Night at Dinner."

From then on, *Zinga Son* progresses from lounge and disco to straight-ahead salsa and funk jams. There are no pauses in between songs, a move that seeks to emulate the dynamics of a DJ set.

Fittingly, Los Amigos changed their notoriously raucous live performances to reflect the new stylistic developments, dividing gigs into two defined sections. And although electronica had become an important part of their identity, they insisted on reproducing their complex sonics with live instruments.

"There's a lounge side to us that we really love," Pardo explained. "We begin with a lounge set of our soft tunes, and then we follow that up with a second, funkier dance set. Most DJs cannot put together a show with a live band, and most live bands cannot switch genres like a DJ. We are somewhere in the middle. We want to be a band and a DJ at the same time." He pauses and thinks for a minute.

"Just like Pérez Prado was," he adds.

Pardo: *Our biggest goal during the last couple of years was to gain some sort of autonomy as a group. The music industry is planned for musicians to be dependent on somebody else's money. Fortunately, that's not the case with us anymore. We don't depend on a record company as such. We have our own studio and book our own gigs. We love it. We don't owe anything to anyone. We do as we please.*

Things get tense when we have financial problems. If there are no shows, there's no money. It's true what they say about the big corporations: the problems arise when there's either too much or too little money. We're in a very optimistic mood right now. We feel like we own our future. Whatever our next album turns out to be, the master will be ours. We have achieved a certain level of integrity as a band. Our relationship with [label] Luaka Bop has been too good to be true. We have nothing bad to say about them. Through David Byrne, we were introduced in this country not as a rock en español *band but as a World-music group. That was extremely beneficial to us. We haven't broken our relationship with them and are not actively looking for another record deal. But the era of the record label is gone. The game needs to be designed in a different way. Luaka Bop used to pay for the albums, promotion, and music videos. Now we're doing all of that ourselves.*

Our plan is to continue making music for many years to come. Playing and touring is just grand, but we need to make more money if we want to keep doing this for another fifteen years. It's about time we buy our own homes. We make no money whatsoever on album sales and we split the publishing advances among the six of us. I may be the main songwriter in the band, but I'm happy sharing my income with the guys. If there's animosity within the group, then Los Amigos ceases to exist. If Los Amigos ceases to exist, then there's no one to play my songs. It's like a circle.

We divide the work among the six of us so that no one feels insecure about his place within the group. It's more like a company now. We play a lot of gigs, release the occasional compilation, and record jingles for commercials. Contrary to the idealized image of the musician who travels first class, we cut corners in order to make touring viable for us. Sometimes we take flights with many stops in order to save on the fares, or we'll share hotel rooms. We're cautious in our management because we can't stop playing live. Fortunately, the magic is still there. We may argue from time to time, but as soon as we're onstage playing, the discussion is over and we're having a great time.

To this day, my two favorite Amigos albums are Venezuelan gozadera *and* Zinga son. *Zinga was the kind of album that we had wanted to make for years.* Gozadera *captured a moment that was just perfect for us. We were discovering the cha cha cha and the bossa nova—and you can actually hear the sense of discovery in those songs. All those influences are more internalized in our subsequent albums.*

As long as we continue playing together, we will continue changing our sound because we're always exposed to new sounds. Trying out new sounds becomes more fun the moment you become used to working in the studio. Right now we're really into the eighties funk of Prince and the more experimental vein of Stereolab. I hope we'll always be thirsty for new musical experiences.

Los Amigos' darkest hour came when we moved to New York. The band was very popular in Venezuela at the time, and you could say that we were spoiled. All of a sudden, we lost our manager and realized that we had become virtual unknowns again. We had a meeting in Central Park that could have very well ended with Los Amigos disbanding.

But then we remembered our beginnings, when we did this for fun and nobody was telling us what to do or how to do it. We decided to carry on.

One of my happiest moments with the band was a gig in front of two hundred people at a New York club. The audience was just connected with everything that was happening onstage. Suddenly the light went out and the crowd stayed there, waiting for the power to come back. It was like playing a party in somebody's home. Just like when we started out fifteen years ago.

Juana Molina

WHEN ARGENTINE ACTRESS Juana Molina announced that she
was quitting her highly successful television show in favor of
a career in music, the Buenos Aires media reacted with a collective smile of condescension—then proceeded to ignore her
excellent debut album, 1996's *Rara* (Weird).
But Molina persevered. By the time she released her second effort, *Segundo* (Second), she had found a unique sound,
juxtaposing her lilting voice to delicately layered soundscapes
informed by electronica.
The record received positive reviews in mainstream U.S.
publications such as *Entertainment Weekly* and *Rolling Stone*.
Molina was also enjoying a cult following in Japan, where she
tours frequently.
The release of *Tres cosas* (Three Things), her latest collection of esoteric ballads, coincided with a tour as the opening
act for David Byrne. Even the snotty Argentine press began
to admit that the former television comedian was a force to
be reckoned with.
"In the end, things happened exactly the way I wanted,"
Molina told me from England in 2004, where she had recently
completed a series of enthusiastically received shows. "Slowly
but steadily. Brick by brick."
Molina pointed out that she had no idea why her music
struck a nerve in this country as opposed to Latin America—
the obvious candidate for her brand of poetic ambient-pop.
"Maybe the fact that I grew up listening to British groups like
Yes and King Crimson is reflected in my belief that the music
is always more important than the words," she ventured.
"The lyrics occupy an important place in the songs that I
write, but they're not essential in order to enjoy the music."
Rara was produced by Gustavo Santaolalla—a collaboration that did not quite work out on a personal level, although

it managed to produce some terrific music. The title track suggested the lyrical subtlety of Suzanne Vega.

Cuando viajo para casa en colectivo
No tengo nada en que pensar
Y si acaso veo un auto igual al suyo
Yo me pregunto dónde está.

When I'm on the bus that takes me home
I have nothing to think about
And if I spot a car that looks like his
I wonder where he could be.

Santaolalla had insisted that Molina form a band, a concept she didn't feel comfortable with. In the late nineties, she moved with her husband and daughter to Los Angeles, where she collaborated with local songwriters and began recording the demos that would become *Segundo*.

Her second effort revealed more of the real Molina. It was subtle and introspective. There was no band to speak of, but rather a woman, her voice, and a battery of electronic equipment. *Tres cosas* was even more enjoyable. It proved, once and for all, that melody was hardly her forte. Molina relied on the minimalism of her guitar lines, the seductive purring of her sleepy voice, and moody computerized textures in order to turn her barely finished tracks into dreamy miniatures.

As she delved into the world of live concerts, Molina realized that she had an additional obstacle to surmount: a bad case of stage fright.

During her television years, she would hide beneath a number of grotesquely exaggerated characters based on Argentine archetypes. Playing her songs in a live setting was an altogether different—and more vulnerable—scenario. "I had an issue with that and I had to work on it," she admitted. "I would be playing live, and my mind would begin to draw absurd conclusions about what the audience was thinking. At that moment, you think you know everything, and you become horrified about the truths that you are allegedly discovering. That doesn't happen to me anymore. Playing frequently has definitely helped."

The singer's Los Angeles debut at a small venue called McCabe's was a disaster. Molina began this solo show playing with the wrong guitar—then stopped the song in the middle so that she could get the correct instrument. Things went downhill from there. She forgot the lyrics to some of her songs, and looked so out of control that the resulting performance evoked a combination of pity and morbid fascination. Fortunately, she put her comedic talents to good use when trying to connect with the capacity audience in English. And although her material shines when performed in Spanish, her few English songs had a strange charm to them that recalled Astrud Gilberto's wispy *bossa novas*. Still, the following morning, Molina vowed never to perform live again. A few months later, she packed her bags and returned to Argentina.

Molina did continue performing in Buenos Aires, but was still unable to shake off her paralyzing bouts of stage fright. Her low point happened during a Buenos Aires show at a venue with poor sound quality. "Hours before the show, I was doing my sound check in front of people who I thought were regular customers getting something to drink. As it turns out, they were the fans who had come to see the show. And they got to see the failed sound check, my bad temper, and patent disappointment. The sound was just impossible."

Molina had such a bad time during the subsequent show that she decided to end the performance prematurely by triggering a loop from one of her albums and leaving the stage. She then realized that she had nowhere to go.

"The show ended with me standing against a wall, my back to the audience, waiting for everyone to leave the premises," she told me. "It was the worst nightmare of my entire life."

She added quickly, "Nothing like that will ever happen to me again."

Until recently, Molina performed in concert accompanied by fellow Argentine multi-instrumentalist Alejandro Franov. Franov added the right touches of texture and dissonance to Molina's sparse electronica miniatures, and the duo generated the instrumental alchemy of a live band.

But Franov lost his passport a few days before a scheduled 2004 tour and Molina was forced to reconfigure her show as a solo performance. "Now I am truly free," she smiled. "I think fate was trying to tell me that I needed to take that one brave step forward and get to know myself. I don't even need to have someone by my side in order to know that I exist."

Molina tested the new solo show in Buenos Aires, in front of 1,300 of her newly acquired Argentine fans. Franov was in the audience. "At the end of the show he came to congratulate me," she says, her voice beaming with pride. "And he told me, 'You did it, Juana. You did it.'"

This change had a wonderful effect on Molina. I saw her perform at Los Angeles' Troubadour, and her one-woman show was more riveting than anything she had done before. Watching her work with a battery of electronic equipment was like witnessing the act of an expert illusionist. She was particularly dexterous about combining instantly manufactured loops with the live element of her performance, adding dissonant keyboard solos and bizarre vocal effects to the mix. During *Segundo*'s "Misterio uruguayo" (Uruguayan Mystery), she triggered an impromptu loop of her own vocals, then sang the song's wry lyrics harmonizing with herself. The moment was overwhelmingly rich and sensuous.

Molina could very well be the bravest woman in Latin music. She could exploit her physical beauty if she so wanted, but instead projects an image of ethereal austerity. She could draw from her gifts for comedy, but her material emphasizes gravity and contemplation over humor. She could hide her obvious shyness beneath a full-fledged band, but instead has opted to go solo—with courage and pride.

Nortec Collective

Bostich.

SOMETIME DURING THE late nineties, Ramón Amezcua had a revelation. A friend of his by the name of Pepe Mogt had given him a tape with samples culled from the demos that local *banda sinaloense* and *norteño* groups in their native Tijuana had recorded in order to get local gigs at night clubs and seafood restaurants. *Norteño* music is defined by its bouncy beat and melodious accordion licks. *Banda sinaloense* favors a more majestic, larger-than-life sound, combining massive brass sections with syncopated snare drumming.

The idea was to take those samples and transpose them to the beat-friendly field of electronica—creating something that would be altogether new.

An orthodontist by trade, Amezcua was a music fan obsessed with early electronica artists such as Kraftwerk and Klaus Schulze that he would hear on American radio stations during his teenage years. He had begun dabbling with sequencers, turntables, and rhythm machines in the early nineties. He followed Mogt's advice and realized that something special happened when he combined these two disparate worlds.

"I sampled the virtuoso beats of the *banda sinaloense* snare drums and processed them through various synthesizer filters, both digital and analog," he recalls. "The groove was the same, but the overall effect became more rhythmic, and eventually turned into something new. It was a fascinating transformation."

Amezcua wasn't the only DJ to receive that infamous tape. In fact, Mogt gave it to various Tijuana DJs and music makers, unleashing a chain reaction of parallel experimentation that resulted in the formation of a sound collective known as Nortec.

The collective's original members included Bostich (Amezcua's stage name), Terrestre, Hiperboreal, Panóptica, Plankton Man, Clorofila, and Fussible. The latter is none other than Mogt himself.

"Fussible was the innovator, the one who came up with the idea and found the actual samples," clarifies Ignacio Chávez Uranga, a.k.a. Plankton Man. "But Bostich was the first one to record the genre's anthem, a cool track called 'Polaris.' We think of him as the Godfather of Nortec. It's very similar to what Talvin Singh did in England—bringing the influence of his Indian origins into electronica. We do the same, only that we mix the beats with tasty Mexican sounds. When you listen to our stuff, you can feel the Latin spice in it."

Perhaps because Nortec is such a clear encapsulation of border culture and its contrasting elements, artists from other disciplines were eager to join the movement. Thus, the Nortec aesthetic was enhanced with the creative presence of graphic designers, architects, painters, and theorists.

In the beginning, Nortec was a local phenomenon, and its raves were attended by a few hundred fans. It wasn't long, however, before the American mainstream came knocking on the collective's door. In 2001, Palm Pictures released Nortec's debut disc. Entitled *The Tijuana Sessions Vol. 1*, it included tracks by all of its members. The record has enjoyed critical acclaim, including articles and reviews in a number of mainstream publications worldwide.

Most importantly, Nortec has managed the seemingly impossible: the creation of an altogether new subgenre in the world of Latin music. There's nothing obvious about the way the original *banda* and *norteño* samples have been manipulated. In fact, when you experience Nortec for the first time, it's hard to identify the syncopated bits of tubas and snare drums, as well as the occasional outbursts of accordion riffs.

"We have fused *banda sinaloense* with electronica, but this is not the classic *banda* we're talking about," explains Amezcua. "The local bands here in Tijuana are influenced by other styles as well, including cumbia and even salsa, and that shows in their music. In a way, what we do is the fusion of another fusion."

Listening to "Polaris," the opening track of the Palm compilation, it is hard not to be swept away by the remarkable sonic imagination of Bostich. In his able hands, the original tuba samples become psychedelic roars that suggest mystery and decadence. Add the nervy syncopation of a neurotic snare drum and the ritualistic pulse of a fat rhythm machine, and "Polaris" could easily be the soundtrack to an imaginary movie depicting the debauchery of the Roman Empire. Caligula on electronics is an apt description of Nortec as experienced by Bostich. Bring on the dancing elephants.

There's something exhilarating about the track, the feeling that you are witnessing the creation of something entirely new. "Polaris" also serves as a bridge into the idiosyncratic world of Nortec, with its occasional moments of abstract sonics and its jarring combination of natural sounds with artificial beats.

Besides creating some pretty groundbreaking dance music, Nortec delivers a perfect aural representation of the border culture that finds young Latinos growing up ready to embrace both the Latino and Anglo sensibilities. This is, perhaps, one of the main reasons why Nortec has been accepted by many a dance music fan—regardless of his or her ethnic origins. The project has also helped to bring the cult universe of electronica closer to the Mexican mainstream. It's a reverse crossover, if you wish.

"We were afraid that people would laugh at us," remembers Amezcua, who performed his first Nortec set for a crowd of fifty people in June 1999. "But the crowd was visibly moved. Now we get about four thousand people every time we do a rave."

"I've seen young couples in some of the biggest raves dancing to our music *quebradita* style," says Uranga. "It's an interesting contrast to see, this traditional dance coupled with music that sounds so futuristic."

"We're going to play in other places besides the big cities," says Amezcua with pride. "We're going to Aguas Calientes and Toluca, places where you would never expect to find a rave. And still, when you get there, you see that every town has its own DJs, and they all know who you are."

It took the Nortec Collective five years to release a new effort. "The future of Nortec depends solely on us," emphasized Amezcua at the time. "Palm has been really gracious about not telling us what to do. And we're not about to release tons and tons of new Tijuana sessions. We're really focused on the quality of the music. We will put something out only if we're really pleased with the results."

Released in 2005, *Tijuana Sessions Vol. 3* is every bit as good as its predecessor—if not better. "At first it was really hard for us to grapple with the fact that we had to go beyond the experiment that our first album was all about," Amezcua told me during a conversation we had a couple of weeks before the new album was released to unanimous critical praise. "The thing is, we couldn't really continue experimenting on top of the experiments. What we all saw as our only option was to enrich our established sound without letting it become a formula."

Indeed, some of the tracks on the new album could very well be outtakes from the first one. But the collective's new creative breakthrough came with the decision to invite *banda* musicians to perform live in the studio. The presence of trumpets, guitars, tubas, and trombones make for a fuller, more mature sound.

"It was a different way of making music for us," Amezcua points out. "Until now, we all made music on our own, working on a laptop at home. Bringing outside instrumentalists to a studio enriched our style. It gave us new sounds, as well as new ways of manipulating those sounds."

The recording of the new album began with an informal get together during which the collective's members played their latest tracks to each other. Each member of the new Nortec—Bostich, Clorofila, Fussible, Hiperboreal, and Panóptica—had an allotment of three tracks for "Vol. 3."

"There were a lot of surprises," recalls Amezcua. "Pepe [Fussible] brought this pop track called 'Tijuana Makes Me Happy.' It was extremely accessible without losing the Nortec element. Clorofila followed an altogether different path. His songs were funky and humorous. Roberto [Panóptica] had been working with [alt-country group] Calexico. Their collaboration added a different mood to the record."

On his end, Amezcua wanted to explore his obsession with the aural universe of Herb Alpert and the Tijuana Brass. Through Tijuana singer Luis Elorza (whose deadpan vocalizing on "Tijuana Makes Me Happy" is one of the album's highest points), he was introduced to Jorge González ("El Zorrita"), a fiery trumpet player who reminded Amezcua of the Tijuana Brass touch and ended up performing on many of the album's tracks.

Terrestre and Plankton Man had left the group after the collective's success generated a wave of internal turmoil. "It was like a giant snowball at first," explains Amezcua. "When it all started, we just weren't ready for this kind of success. And we argued about who would be the collective's protagonist, which in our case is unimportant."

According to Amezcua, the members of Nortec worked with the same manager, but the disputes began when they were flooded with invididual offers to participate in other artists' albums, perform solo concerts, and record on their own. The departure of two founding members functioned as a cleansing of sorts for the collective.

"The remaining five of us have stuck together," he says. "We still have differences stemming from time management—which gigs to accept, which invitations to accept when we're offered to record a commercial jingle or sell our music to the movies. Fortunately, we use the Internet as a medium to discuss all these issues, and it has worked out for us."

But the current members make it a point not to allow themselves to be engulfed by the trappings of fame. "We're always teasing each other about our 'techno star' lifestyles," Amezcua laughs. "It's funny how easy it is for the autograph signing and the meeting of rock stars to go to your head. In my case, I just don't like that lifestyle. All of us made it a point to continue leading a normal existence."

Does that mean that the one and only Bostich, leader of the visionary Nortec Collective, is still a practicing dentist?

"Of course I am," he says proudly. "I lost about 80 percent of my patients when the first record came out and I was always touring, but I've slowly managed to get my clientele back. Why would I stop doing something that I love so much? Besides, you can find inspiration for your music anywhere. Even at the dentist's office."

And do the patients bring demos of their own?

"They do," he admits. "I'm afraid some of them are not very good."

Bajofondo Tango Club and Gotan Project

Bajofondo Tango Club. © Javier Ghoghos

THE MUSIC COMING out of Gustavo Santaolalla's Echo Park studio sounds like nothing you have ever heard before. Sure, the plump, electronically generated beat brings to mind the manic intensity of drum+bass. Underneath its fury, however, lies the unmistakable sound of the *bandoneón*, the accordion-like instrument that defines Argentine tango and its bitter nostalgia. Languid and energetic, uplifting and morbid at the same time, the combination of sounds is simply bewitching. It's 2002 and the Bajofondo Tango Club has just been born.

To Santaolalla, who's predominantly known for his production work in the Latin rock field, the combination of tango and electronica marks an exciting new direction in his career as a music maker. In the seventies, while still in his teens and living in his native Argentina, Santaolalla made history by creating Arco Iris, one of the first bands to fuse rock 'n' roll with a Latin tinge. After moving to the United States in the early eighties, Santaolalla and creative partner Aníbal Kerpel established their new identity by helming seminal efforts in the Latin rock field. This led to the creation of the duo's own label, Surco, which enjoys a distribution deal with Universal Music. Now, the Bajofondo Tango Club reveals Santaolalla as a key figure in the development of Latin electronica. It also signifies the birth of Vibra, a Surco imprint devoted solely to the electronica landscape.

Based on its aesthetic merits alone, the record was likely to cause a stir not only in the relatively conservative circles of Latin music, but also in the international electronica community, which is always thirsty for novel experiences and fresh ways of combining the old and the new.

Santaolalla, who was fifty at the time of this interview, told me that he discovered tango, the quintessential musical expression of his native land, late in his life.

"I was always attracted to tango, but I never felt the urge to experiment with it," he explained. "In my case, at least, I needed to be of a certain age in order to be able to appreciate it. Something I've discovered through the making of this project is that the true understanding of tango has a lot to do with owning your own share of memories and experiences. I've always thought that the sight of a child singing tangos is nothing short of horrifying."

The original idea for a tango collective came to Santaolalla in the late nineties. The producer was listening to an album by Portishead and realized that some of the British trip-hop group's soundscapes reminded him of the old tangos that he heard growing up in the suburbs of Buenos Aires.

"I thought there was a moment in one of their songs that was very melancholy and tango-like," he recalled. "I started to experiment with that, talking to friends about it."

Santaolalla was quickly seduced by the idea of mixing such an old-fashioned genre with cutting edge electronica—partly because such a project would give him the kind of creative outlet that producing other people's work could not provide.

"A couple of years ago, I realized that I had two options," Santaolalla said in between recording sessions. "The way my life is structured, it was simply impossible to form a band, record an album, and tour behind it. So, I could altogether abandon my own music making, or invent new ways of expressing my ideas."

In true Portishead fashion, Santaolalla's first experiments were influenced by the trip-hop genre, which anchors its nocturnal mood on slow, elegant beats and elaborate atmospherics. Eventually, the producer focused his attention on the more upbeat, dynamic compositions of tango master Astor Piazzolla, and decided to switch gears and delve into the frantic polyrhythms of drum+bass, a more dance-oriented style. "That's when Bajofondo really came together," he emphasized. "At that moment, I decided to create a collective of likeminded musicians, partners in crime who would bring their own point of view to the project."

Santaolalla first put these ideas into practice through his work writing the soundtrack for the Marcelo Piñeyro film *Plata Quemada*. This was the music that I heard that morning in Echo Park—realizing instantly that I was witnessing the birth of a new musical style. But the director of the film ultimately rejected the music and Santaolalla was free to transform it into an independent project.

Following a similar methodology as the Nortec Collective, Santaolalla made a list of possible conspirators and invited them to record their own take on the electro-tango concept. He flew to Spain, where he met with Juan Campodónico, former guitarist for the Uruguayan band Peyote Asesino (which Santaolalla had produced), now an adventurous record producer living in Madrid. Campodónico loved the Bajofondo concept and moved to Los Angeles for a month to create the sonic blueprint of the project.

"It took a while for us to get it together," admitted Santaolalla. "You can't just play a minor key melody and slap a groove and a *bandoneón* on top of it. For the recipe to succeed, you need equal doses of respect and irreverence."

Santaolalla and Campodónico continued to sell the Bajofondo idea to fellow musicians and producers. Dozens of them offered to participate, which explains why the finished product, a combination of buoyant instrumental tracks and heart-wrenching songs, brims with creativity. Argentine soundtrack composer Emilio Kauderer and Uruguayan singer/songwriter Jorge Drexler—who penned "Perfume," the collective's *bona fide* anthem—were also recruited.

"I think the Bajofondo Tango Club has brought some much-needed heart to the technology of today's music," Kauderer told me. "An instrument like the *bandoneón* is simply irreplaceable. It adds a certain strength and passion to the music, something the machines cannot provide."

The Uruguay-Argentina connection was no coincidence. Like many tango connoisseurs, Santaolalla sees tango as the product of the *Río de la Plata*, the river that separates the two South American countries infused with the same quirky aesthetic and wistful outlook on life. (The Argentine-Uruguayan connection is also at the core of two Santaolalla-produced rock bands, Bersuit Vergarabat and La Vela Puerca.)

Listening to the opening bars of "Perfume" for the first time, you might easily think that it is a traditional tango tune, perhaps a newly recorded version of a decades-old standard.

"Perfume" begins with the smoky, near-masculine growl of Adriana Varela—the foremost tango vocalist of the last fifteen years. A lilting acoustic guitar accompanies her languid reading of the song's bittersweet lyrics, typical of tango's darkly erotic cosmovision.

But then, Varela's voice is suddenly coupled with shimmering keyboard effects. And when the inevitable *bandoneón* finally comes into the picture, it is backed by a thumping house beat that only grows in intensity as the song progresses.

"Santaolalla and Campodónico have a keen understanding of the *mugre*, the grayness and dirt that permeates both

Buenos Aires and Montevideo," Varela told me during a telephone conversation from her home in Argentina. "And they
chose not to hide it. There are no masks here. That's why this
particular fusion has not ended up sounding pretentious or
downright ridiculous."

Varela, who made a name for herself performing a more
traditional brand of tango, says that her fans have wholeheartedly embraced her participation in Bajofondo—in fact, she
regards this project as a natural continuation of her creative
journey.

"Both Santaolalla and I come from the rock generation
that came of age during the seventies. We look for that which
is revealing, not complacent. And that's something you cannot buy. You either carry it in your blood, or you don't."

The nocturnal atmospherics that define Campodónico's
trashy version of the standard "Naranjo en flor" (Blossoming
Orange Tree) with its half-sung, half-spoken female vocals, or
Santaolalla's brooding instrumental "Bruma" (Mist) helped
make Bajofondo a cult hit in Argentina and Europe. A reluctant Universal Latino agreed to release it domestically after the
album experienced success as an import.

"I guess I realized that there was something special about
Bajofondo when I went to [record store] Amoeba and found
it in their list of recommended albums," recounted an amused
Santaolalla. "Then I went to Virgin Megastore, and they had
import copies in the listening station. Clearly, this is happening based solely on the strength of the music."

Just don't mention the Gotan Project. The collective from
Paris, France, has also revisited tango as an electro-friendly
genre, albeit with a more cosmopolitan, less authentic sound.

Some might even say that Gotan got there first. Its appropriately titled debut, *La revancha del tango* (Tango's Revenge), was released before the Bajofondo record. "It's like a stigma," admitted Santaolalla. "Every time I talk about Bajofondo, Gotan will inevitably come up. I can't start telling everyone I know that I've been working on this stuff for over four years. Besides, it often happens that a concept is floating somewhere in the ether, and two people grab it at the same time. Artists tend to function like radars that way."

Varela, whose participation in Bajofondo is limited to singing a couple of songs, is more openly dismissive of the competition. "What they do is more *project* than *gotan*," she says in her flavorful Argentine accent. "We're exactly the opposite. We made a tango record that happens to be electronic."

Rumor has it that a meeting was held between both groups. Santaolalla's approach was conciliatory; he proposed a collaboration. Gotan fans see this as a maneuver on his part to legitimize his project. Bajofondo fans regard Santaolalla's gesture as a gentlemanly invitation for musical peace. In any case, the members of Gotan allegedly refused the offer. "Too late," they told him—firmly and politely.

Santaolalla sees Bajofondo as the beginning of something that could easily develop a life of its own. "We could have a Bajofondo disc that's strictly devoted to dance, and another one with chill-out stuff," he said enthusiastically. "We could have Bajofondo concerts and Bajofondo DJ nights. That's the beauty of this project. It could easily branch out into a lot of different things."

�֍

Through the combined efforts of Bajofondo and Gotan, electro-tango became an accepted subgenre of Latintronica—a reminder that Latin rock will continue to branch out into new, exciting formats.

The competition between the two collectives became inevitable when both performed concerts in Los Angeles within the same couple of years.

Lit by beams of silvery light as they played their instruments with motionless restraint, the members of Gotan looked like the characters of an old, monochrome movie—distant and nostalgic. The group's performance came to life halfway through the show, when a transparent screen showing artsy video images in front of the musicians was dropped in favor of a more natural setting. It was then that the band gave free reign to its more raucous side—a combination of bittersweet textures informed by fiery touches of violin, thorny piano lines, and the occasional presence of a female vocalist.

Moving away from the decadence of Buenos Aires tango, Gotan ventured into Argentine folklore by intertwining a rootsy rhythm reminiscent of the traditional chacarera with funky artificial beats. This daring fusion—and a shimmering encore that included the brand new "La cruz del sur" (The Southern Cross) and an intriguing take on Gato Barbieri's "Last Tango in Paris"—were promising enough to forgive the colorless repetitiveness that afflicts some of the collective's material.

Bajofondo's performance was a different story.

A scratchy old vinyl gave way to a thumping drum machine. Delicate clusters of piano morphed into liquid-sounding electronica effects. A quartet of guitar, upright bass, violin, and *bandoneón* was framed by a semicircle of two DJs and a female VJ who projected loops of old black-and-white film onto a giant screen. The live reading of "Naranjo en flor" was wonderfully iconoclastic. Varela was absent and "Perfume" was performed with her prerecorded voice—the show's only flaw.

Watching a joyful Santaolalla performing live was a rare treat. It's easy to forget that this respected producer began his career as a guitarist with Arco Iris. No wonder he looked right at home onstage, jumping up and down to his visionary tango beat.

Gustavo Santaolalla

GUSTAVO SANTAOLALLA closes his eyes and contorts his face in a frightening grimace, lost in the rapture of the music. Astride a rolling chair, he cranks up the volume, taps the rhythm with his foot, and shakes his head spastically. Now he's doing some air guitar and chanting along in a strident falsetto—just like a lonely teenage boy locked in his room, dreaming dreams of rock 'n' roll grandeur.

But this isn't the bedroom of a suburban adolescent. In fact, we're inside an Echo Park studio, the heart of the kingdom where Santaolalla and his partner, Aníbal Kerpel, record and produce some of Latin rock's most innovative artists. It's also the headquarters of Surco, the duo's record company, which currently enjoys a five-year, multimillion-dollar deal with Universal Music Group. This is where Santaolalla has staged his ascent. He is now the magus, the alchemist, the guru of *rock en español*.

Today, on a crisp autumn morning in 1999, Santaolalla is excited because he's found yet another artist with something special—Erica García, an Argentine rocker with the voice of a seraph. Then again, he's always excited about something new. He continues to cultivate working relationships with musicians he considers important, but he's always on the lookout for fresh new voices. That probably accounts for why Santaolalla and Kerpel look like a couple of guys in their early forties, though they're actually about to turn fifty.

Surprisingly, Santaolalla finds the time to be a music geek, avidly collecting anything related to popular music, and he's known about García since her days ten years ago in Buenos Aires, when she sang with the punk group Mata Violeta. Santaolalla even owns bootleg live videos of the band, and he has wanted to produce a García solo record for a long time.

So delighted is Santaolalla about *Amorama* that he makes me listen to yet another track, though the vocals are far from finished. Santaolalla's biggest obsession is creating the perfect vocal line, or, as he explains in technese, "I'm a freak about doing the vocal comps." He records his singers on a dozen takes for each tune, then begins the laborious process of editing words—make that syllables, even microbeats of vowels and consonants—stitching the minuscule moments from each take that he hears as the absolute best. So if García sings "*el amor*," "*el*" will be culled from, say, take 12, "*a*" from take 3, "*mo*" from take 11, and "*or*" from take 12 again.

In order for me to appreciate why vocal comps are of such crucial importance to the finished product, Santaolalla plays a García song with one of the regular vocal takes mixed in, then plays the same tune with the finished comps. The difference is remarkable. Then I listen to the song while looking at a computer monitor where a needle indicates (much as in an Avid movie-editing system) the vast number of vocal edits that have shaped this particular mix.

"I'm showing you the secrets," he sighs, a hint of regret in his voice. "I'm taking you backstage and showing you how the rabbits are pulled out of the magician's hat."

Then Erica García enters the studio. She gives us all a fleshy sort of smile, showing a lot of perfect white teeth and giving Santaolalla a soft peck on the cheek. She's part Barbarella, part Lolita, a playful little girl hidden in the body of a grown woman. She sits down, throws her purse on the floor, and listens to the new mixes with palpable enthusiasm.

Santaolalla wants me to like García. He champions all of his artists passionately, and no doubt because he's experienced my admiration for many of them, he does a pretty convincing job of showing me how superb each one of his new projects is.

So García and Santaolalla play another song for me, only this one doesn't have vocals on it yet, just a soft, lilting cushion of keyboards, guitars, and drums. And García and Santaolalla sing the tune for me, live, harmonizing together, García taking the spotlight, Santaolalla complementing her. They've chosen a tune that talks about a woman loving a man, but deals with it honestly, with plenty of contradiction, not with the usual clichés that you hear on your average pop tune. No, García sings about doing the sweetest things to her beau while stepping on him, *because* she adores him so. The bitter and the sweet, the Eros and the Thanatos, the virgin and the whore.

The song ends. García exhales her last breath, then there's this movie moment, the "it is accomplished" sort of thing where she looks around her, at me and Kerpel and Santaolalla, and smiles mischievously.

I tap her on the shoulder.

"Who did you write this for?"

She smiles nervously. "Well, you know . . ."

Santaolalla says sternly, "You don't have to answer."

"Why are you getting involved in this?" I suddenly bark back at him. "I'm asking *her*, not you."

For a brief moment, there's an expression of utter disbelief on Santaolalla's face. "What do you mean, 'why am I getting involved?'" he says, heatedly. "She's my artist!"

"They always ask me that," says Erica, in a futile, conciliatory digression. "They want to know how, where, and when I write my songs. They ask me these real specific things."

"Of course we do," I say. "We want to see Picasso at work. We want to study Einstein's brain."

"I don't believe this!" screams Santaolalla. "We get together. We take all of our clothes off. We get butt-naked just for you. And as if that wasn't enough, now you wanna stick your finger up our asses!" Loud laughter ensues.

It is no coincidence that Santaolalla's name appears so many times throughout this book. He has unified the entire movement by becoming involved, at one point or another, with the majority of the genre's major players: Café Tacvba, Julieta Venegas, Molotov, Maldita Vecindad, Fabulosos Cadillacs, Caifanes, Juana Molina, and Bajofondo Tango Club. And by developing the career of Colombian pop-rocker Juanes, he has been responsible for the emergence of one of Latin music's most commercially successful artists. He has also composed the soundtracks for quality art films such as *Amores Perros*, *21 Grams*, and *The Motorcycle Diaries*. He has collaborated with the Kronos Quartet and vocalist Dawn Upshaw, recorded a 2005 tango revival *a la* Buena Vista Social Club, and even launched a book imprint devoted to music-related projects. The man's artistic hunger is limitless.

I discovered Santaolalla sometime in the midnineties, when I became acquainted with albums by Tacvba, Molotov, and Molina—all in the span of a few months. Strangely enough, these disparate records sounded alike in a weird sort of way. While the stylistic directions they followed were in sharp contrast, there was something about the spatial relationships of the elements within the music, a three-dimensional feeling about the productions, that made you understand that this was the work of a producer of the caliber of Brian Eno or Daniel Lanois.

I realized then that there was magic in Santaolalla, for every artist he laid his hands on emerged a better musician. He'd been instrumental in the development of Latin rock not as a performer, but as a facilitator, liberator, and discoverer of potential. He was the man who allowed Tacvba, Venegas, Molotov, and Bersuit Vergarabat to transcend their stereotyped roles and become something far more interesting than a bunch of Latin American *rockeros*.

"He's not a 'musical director' type of producer," Café Tacvba's Del Real told me. "He listens to the group's music, and becomes one with its philosophy and its future direction. He literally becomes another band member."

Santaolalla's artistry as a composer and performer can be best appreciated on 1998's *Ronroco*. A collection of twelve delicate, impressionistic vignettes, it relies mostly on South American string instruments such as the *charango* and the *ronroco*. Half the tunes are completely abstract, creating evocative washes of sound that rely solely on mood. The other half consists of gorgeous melodies, lullabies for the soul, mesmerizing in their construction and perfection.

"It's entirely acoustic," says Santaolalla with a mischievous grin. "No electronic bullshit. And it wasn't recorded overnight. It took thirteen years to finish."

"The first half of the album," adds Kerpel, "was recorded in a living room, with a single microphone going into a cassette recorder." Santaolalla's magic did the rest, with various overdubs and an overall digital treatment of the sound.

Ronroco is a very short album, and it introduces the rock listener to the bridge between Santaolalla the rocker and the folklore of his native Argentina. It is the latter that explains why, in his role as a producer, he has encouraged his artists to heed the musical roots of their respective countries; Santaolalla's productions exploit the electrifying dynamics of rock, but are suffused with the comforting presence of a past well lived.

In Santaolalla's case, this past involves superstardom at a young age.

As a boy in his native Buenos Aires, he listened avidly to his parents' vast, eclectic record collection, which ranged from Nat King Cole and Argentinian tango to folklore legends such as Atahualpa Yupanqui. He started taking guitar lessons at the age of five, formed his first group at eleven, and never looked back.

In the late sixties he was the leader of the pioneering *rock en español* group Arco Iris. The group's sound was deeply influenced by folk and traditional South American music, and Gustavo became a celebrity as its leader.

"In a way, I became very famous too young," he reflects today. "My memories from the Arco Iris days are both good and bad. Generally speaking, the positive memories outweigh the negative ones. Musically, it was the first project where I started to implement my vision and way of doing things. There was an article in an Argentine magazine called *Pelo*—they interviewed me right before I moved to the United States in the early eighties. And the article was named "*Como a destiempo*," meaning that my work always clashed with the trends that were going on at the time. Because I always had ideas that were, somehow, ahead of their time. Conceptually, for instance, Arco Iris was what Café Tacvba is today. It's the same concept. The results were different, obviously. It was a

different era, a different country. We were different people.
But the idea and the thirst for experimentation was the same.
Like *Agitor Lucens* and its instrumental passages."

I asked Santaolalla if he thought that the old Arco Iris
records had withstood the test of time.

"There's a lot of good stuff in there," he answered. "I'm
not going to tell you that it's all good. We had some ten-
minute guitar solos going on. . . . Today, those would be short-
ened. It's the kind of thing you do when you are young. We
didn't have a producer. I produced everything. I was sixteen,
seventeen years old at the time. Arco Iris had a huge hit named
"Mañanas campestres" (Country Mornings). Even taxi driv-
ers in Argentina know that song by heart.

"The memories of Argentina are always in what I'd call
'my hard disc.' They're inside my soul. I take them with me
wherever I go. Sometimes I'll return, mentally speaking, to
some of the places of my youth. It happens late at night, just
before I go to bed. I remember gigs I did with Arco Iris, even
entire tours that we did."

Back then, Kerpel was an ambitious keyboard player with
prog-rock outfit Crucis. But in the late seventies, both musicians migrated to Los Angeles separately, looking for more
opportunities to express themselves far away from the oppression of Argentina's military regime. It was there that they both
met their wives, got married, and formed families, creating
what Santaolalla refers to as "their own tribe."

"I arrived in the United States at the worst possible time,"
he told me. "In Argentina, we belonged to an alternative music
movement that was heavily involved in politics. We didn't
belong to a political party per se, but we were part of the coun-
terculture. Here, on the other hand, the heyday of corporate

rock was taking place. The popular groups of the time were Boston, Styx, Kansas. . . . It was horrible. Then I started reading about the Sex Pistols and all the changes that the punk movement was bringing to music. One night, I went to The Whiskey on the Sunset Strip and saw the Motels in concert. That was it. My life changed. I got a haircut, shaved my beard, and bought myself a suit and some ties."

Soon after, the pair formed the new wave/punk outfit Wet Picnic. "We played a mixture of jazz, punk, and new wave. In 1981, we released a record on the Unicorn label. It got some great press, and a wonderful review in *Billboard* magazine. The other day, I played that old music to some of the musicians who perform with Beck and they flipped. They just loved it. But nothing happened with Wet Picnic. Again, it was ahead of its time. Aníbal and I did a bit of everything in order to make ends meet. At one point, he delivered *The Recycler* in his pickup truck. Eventually, he got a job as a sound engineer in music videos. He also worked as a session musician, playing top-forty music six nights a week all over town, from nightclubs to military bases.

"I spent all of the money that I had brought with me, and then I got the record label to sponsor me while Wet Picnic was happening. I also had another project, a fusion of black music with Latin folklore, like *chacareras* and cumbias. If you listen to those demos today, they sound a little like Jamiroquai. I was about to sign a record deal for that, and it ended up falling apart. At that point, I had a nervous breakdown."

I told Santaolalla that he didn't look like the type who would have a nervous breakdown.

"The same intensity that I channel into creating things, I can channel into destroying myself," he replied. "When this breakdown thing happened, it was pretty bad. I couldn't get out of bed. I was almost hospitalized. Had I stayed in Argentina, I'm pretty sure that I would have become a drug addict and died."

Eventually, Santaolalla and Kerpel received the first offers to produce Maldita Vecindad, Divididos, and Tacvba.

"Producing happened in a very organic way, and it's definitely connected to those obsessive traits of mine. Back then, Wet Picnic was my one and only obsession. And when you focus too much on one thing, you end up destroying it. Metaphorically speaking, it's like beginning with a simple cup of coffee and adding too many things to it. Sugar, salt, and honey. Why not a bit of parsley? You add all these extraneous ingredients to it and it becomes a cup of slimy, undrinkable mud.

"There was a key moment in my life that I think signified my birth as a record producer, and that was in 1984, when I became involved with an album entitled *De Usuahia a la Quiaca* with folk troubadour León Gieco. There was a score of guest musicians on that record, all of them folk artists with a very pure sense of musicality about them. And I just fell in love with the whole process. I loved being in touch with other performers in that way."

Studying Santaolalla's productions, you learn to distinguish his personal touch in all of them. Every sound element that makes up a song is focused and completely present in its texture. "I want my records to jump out of the speakers," he says, citing George Martin, Brian Eno, Mitchell Froom, and Daniel Lanois as defining influences.

"I like to think of myself as the person who cleans the weeds out of the garden and plants a few beautiful flowers," he continues. "I've come to see that there's something intangible about my productions, a specific energy I possess that gets stuck in every one of my jobs.

"Finding an artist you want to produce is a little like falling in love. You must really fall head over heels with what this artist is doing musically. You can't get involved in this if there's not a strong sense of admiration involved. Then you meet the artist and try to decide whether there's good chemistry between the two of you. See if there's a common vision, at least concerning the work that needs to be done. Discipline is another fundamental element for things to work out.

"If all these elements fall into place, then I'm ready to work with the artist in question. That said, there are a number of artists who possess their own identity and original voice, are good human beings, and are diligent when it comes to doing the work, but I don't connect with them on an instinctive level. There's no reasoning behind this, no logical explanation. You either feel somebody's music, or you don't."

Santaolalla emphasized the fact that no studio gimmicks can replace real talent. "Ultimately, the sound is like the makeup on an actor, or the art direction in a movie," he says. "The songs are the thing. If you don't have good songs, there's nothing that can save your ass."

Appendix: More of Rock en Español

Ely Guerra.

THE PREVIOUS CHAPTERS touched on the artists who, in my opinion, are essential for the understanding of *rock en español* and the creative peak it experienced during the last ten years. Fortunately, the genre is rich enough to include a number of others who have also left an indelible mark on the Latin rock landscape. Serious fans should also explore the works mentioned in this appendix. The best albums hereunder are an indispensable addition to any well-rounded *rock en español* collection.

Pedro Aznar

A unique and sensitive singer/songwriter, Argentina's Pedro Aznar gained popularity in the late seventies as a member of the Charly García–fronted supergroup Serú Girán. A student at the prestigious Berklee College of Music, he spent part of the eighties touring and recording with jazz guitarist Pat Metheny. His rootsy "Vidala," which appears on Metheny's 1989 *Letter from Home* album and is inspired by the folk music of South America, stands as one of the most poignant songs in the guitarist's vast oeuvre. In turn, Metheny participated in Aznar's first two solo albums: 1982's *Pedro Aznar* was a rustic affair, marked by intriguing adaptations of the Beatles ("Because"), Maurice Ravel ("Pavane Pour Une Infante Defunte"), and Miles Davis ("Nefertiti"); and 1985's *Contemplación* boasts languid pop songs like "A la hora que se duermen los trenes" (When Trains Fall Asleep) and the gorgeous "Al dolor de mi gente" (To My People's Pain), which showcases Aznar's trademark wordless vocalizing at its most affecting. Aznar has continued releasing worthwile albums without achieving massive popularity.

Recommended

Contemplación (1985)
Cuerpo y alma (1998)

La Banda Elástica

Based out of West Covina in California, *La Banda Elástica* is widely considered by fans to be the Bible of *rock en español*. The magazine's run of back issues constitute an extensive encyclopedia of Latin rock. Current issues provide exposure to new, undiscovered artists. *La Banda* was founded by musician/designer Emilio Morales and his girlfriend, photographer María Madrigal. It began as a fanzine and blossomed during the mid- to late nineties. The articles—written mostly by Latin rock eminence Enrique Blanc—are particularly incisive, whereas Madrigal's photos cast an endearing glance on the evolution of the genre.

Bersuit Vergarabat

The quintessential Argentine group of the new millennium, Bersuit has continued the legacy of Fabulosos Cadillacs as a musically omnivorous band with sociopolitical lyrics. A hugely successful outfit, it has created waves in and out of Argentina through its propensity for scatological humor and all sorts of crass innuendo.

Founded in 1988 by vocalist Gustavo Cordera, Bersuit achieved cult status in Buenos Aires long before Gustavo Santaolalla produced its breakthrough album, 1998's *Libertinaje* (Licentiousness). The record includes "Sr. Cobranza," the cover version of a tune by obscure band Las Manos de Filippi that combines angry political condemnation with over-the-top musicianship. Beginning with a laid-back, contemplative groove, the song slowly builds to an explosive crescendo of rock 'n' roll frenzy and an obscenity-laden attack against the Argentine government and the oppression of Latinos everywhere.

Live, the members of Bersuit are notorious for peforming in their pajamas, exposing their posteriors to the audience while working out extended instrumental jams. If the crowd reacts by booing them, Cordera is known to lash out against the audience, accusing them of being prudish and repressed.

Hijos del culo (Children of the Ass), released in 2000, was Bersuit's best album to date, a kaleidoscopic exploration of the group's many musical fetishes (the Uruguayan carnival rhythm known as *murga*, as well as the working-class-friendly *cumbia*, to name a few), enhanced by a surprisingly mature compositional approach. The album is dedicated to the album title's "Children of the Ass," or, as Cordera explains in the liner notes, "the abandoned ones, the betrayed ones, the forgotten ones, those who were left out of the banquet and expelled from paradise." *Hijos* creates an indelible statement by coupling the band's usual penchant for grotesquerie with tender bits of lyrical poetry—a volatile combination that separates Bersuit from other Latin rock groups. The opening "El gordo motoneta" (Fat Motorcycle Man), the story of a man whose inordinate zest for life renders him both indispensable and repulsive to others, is a veiled homage to producer Santaolalla.

Fueled by the album's success, Bersuit built a studio and recorded the double album/manifesto *La argentinidad al palo* (Argentine to the Max, 2004). Musically, the band continues to explore an exuberant, pan-Latino fusion that can easily switch from a domestic *chacarera* beat to a Mexican *cumbia norteña*. The band lost none of its desire to provoke and disgust, as the disco-tinged "Coger no es amor" (Fucking Is Not Love) would seem to indicate. Hidden beneath the mock–Bee Gees harmonies and the lurid nature of the lyrics, however, lie moments of profound tenderness and compassion such as the heartbreaking ballad "Al olor del hogar" (A Home's Scent, an unusually dispassionate look at growing up poor) and the electronica-informed ode to loneliness "La soledad" (Loneliness). Bersuit's very essence is a paradox—one that continues to inject humor and originality to *rock en español*.

Recommended

Hijos del culo (2000)
La argentinidad al palo vol. 1 (2004)

Rubén Blades

One of Latin music's most talented and timeless songwriters, Panama's Rubén Blades has recorded mostly within the salsa genre—but his incisive lyrics and propulsive melodies owe a lot to a number of pop-rock icons, from Dylan and the Beatles to Sting and Lou Reed.

Blades' early salsa classics recorded for New York's Fania label in the late seventies should delight rock fans with their socially aware message—the disco pastiche "Plástico" is a perfect example of this tendency. *Buscando América* (Searching for America), released in 1984, ups the rock element within a tropical context on provocative jams such as "El Padre Antonio y su monaguillo Andrés" (Father Antonio and His Altar Boy Andrés). One of its songs, the grim "Desapariciones"

(Disappearings), was covered by both Fabulosos Cadillacs and Maná.

During the last decade, Blades has abandoned the traditional structures of Afro-Caribbean music in search of a new, pan-global pop language that incorporates ethnic elements of various cultures with the mature songwriting methods of, say, Peter Gabriel. *Mundo* (World), released in 2002, crystallizes this new language into a cohesive whole.

Recommended

Siembra (1978)
Buscando América (1984)
Mundo (2002)

Bloque

Bloque was an excellent Colombian group boasting the talents of singer/songwriter Iván Benavides and Mayte Montero, the extraordinary *gaita* (South American flute) player of Carlos Vives' *vallenato*-rock band. Initially known as Bloque de Búsqueda, the group released only one album on David Byrne's Luaka Bop label. Interestingly, the record failed to capture the combustible energy of the band's live performances, which mixed tropical idioms with rock bravado. Together with Aterciopelados, Bloque was one of the few groups who were able to create a viable lexicon of Colombian rock.

Recommended

Bloque (1998)

Botellita de Jerez

Botellita de Jerez was a seminal Mexican group founded by Sergio Arau, Armando Vega Gil, and Paco Barrios. Recorded between 1983 and 1987, the group's first three albums preceding the departure of Arau combine a pan-Latino rock fusion with the trio's corrosive sense of humor (the dark "Alármala de Tos" would be subsequently covered by Café Tacvba to great success). The group carried on without Arau but disbanded in 1997 after the release of a live album.

Recommended

La venganza del hijo de Guacarock (1987)

Brazilian Rock

The relationship between Brazilian music and rock could easily be the subject of an entire book. Brazilian music has always been omnivorous by nature and found inspiration in American pop, rock 'n' roll, reggae, and many other idioms.

The velvety *bossa nova*, in turn, has inspired countless Latin rock musicians, from Ely Guerra and Julieta Venegas to Los Amigos Invisibles and Fabulosos Cadillacs.

In the late sixties and early seventies, an entire generation of Brazilian musicians fused rock idioms with the music of their homeland with outstanding results: Milton Nascimento, Caetano Veloso, Jorge Ben Jor, Gilberto Gil, Chico Buarque, Gal Costa, and many others. Interestingly all of these artists continue releasing vital albums to this day—their collective body of work stands as some of the most imaginative music of the twentieth century. Ben Jor caused a stir by mixing the sounds of Brazil with funk and R&B. Cult band Os Mutantes favored a scrumptious brand of Brazilian psychedelia. A number of now-obscure local groups developed successful careers by following the path of progressive rock. Gilberto Gil, Caetano Veloso, and his sister Maria Bethania gained notoriety through the rebellious sound known as *tropicalia.*

Rock was also the starting point of the underrated *Jovem Guarda* movement, which found singers such as Roberto Carlos (later a superstar crooner *a la* Julio Iglesias), Wanderleia, and Erasmo Carlos (no relation to Roberto) performing punchy, guitar-based rock numbers with subtle touches of psychedelia and soul.

In the eighties, a third wave of rock artists gained popularity: Os Paralamas do Suceso, vocalist Rita Lee, Titas, and Skank. The latter favored a raw mix of reggae and punk in its early days, then matured and recorded an homage of sorts to the Beatles' *Revolver* on the excellent 2003 release *Cosmotron.*

Echoes of rock can also be heard on the music of the popular *axé* movement (a radio friendly combination of pop with funk) through the works of talented vocalists such as Daniela Mercury and Ivete Sangalo.

In the nineties, a group of exceptionally talented singer/songwriters became famous through a pan-global sound that had strong rock elements in it: Marisa Monte, percussionist/producer/composer Carlinhos Brown, and Arnaldo Antunes. These three artists got together in 2002 under the name of Tribalistas. The trio's self-titled debut is highly recommended for fans of quality pop-rock.

Perhaps the most intriguing album in the entire Brazilian rock spectrum is the debut by Karnak, a collective of singers and musicians (and even a dog!) who mix every musical genre under the sky in a surprising collection of baroque pop miniatures. Unfortunately, Karnak disbanded after only a couple of albums.

Recommended

Os Mutantes: *Os mutantes* (1968)
Roberto Carlos: *Roberto Carlos* (1970)
Chico Buarque: *Meus caros amigos* (1976)
Milton Nascimento: *Journey to Dawn* (1979)
Os Paralamas do Sucesso: *Big Bang* (1989)
Karnak: *Karnak* (1997)
Tribalistas: *Tribalistas* (2002)
Skank: *Cosmotron* (2003)

Enrique Bunbury

Throughout Latin America and his home country of Spain, singer/songwriter Enrique Bunbury is idolized for his rock star mystique, smoky vocalizing, and plaintive lyrics. He initially gained notoriety with popular hard-rock outfit Héroes del Silencio, but went solo in 1997 with *Radical sonora*, a relatively successful experiment in electronic textures.

Bunbury came of age with his second solo effort, *Pequeño* (Little). The album functions as a Latin rock version of a nostalgic European art movie, complete with brassy moments of circus euphoria, blood dripping ballads of metaphysical nostalgia, and nocturnal hymns that conclude with the sound of screaming seagulls and waves crashing against the shore of a beach somewhere in Europe.

Bunbury's fusion of disparate elements (flamenco, arena rock, middle Eastern sounds, ranchera pathos, and tango mystique) continued on 2002's *Flamingos*. In 2004, he crammed the two-disc epic *El viaje a ninguna parte* (Journey to Nowhere) with so much color, poetry, and texture that the resulting collection may prove to be an overwhelming experience should you try to digest it in one sitting. Like Manu Chao, Bunbury sees himself as a member of an imaginary troupe that wanders around the world in search of romance and inspiration. He enhances the record's carnivalesque vibe with instrumental touches that are alternately humorous and poignant, like the South American *charango* on the rollicking "Que tengas suertecita" (May You Have Good Luck), or a jazzy trumpet on the nocturnal "Voces de tangos" (Tango Voices). Bunbury is also one of the genre's most compelling live performers. Catch him in concert if you can, or listen to his *Pequeño cabaret ambulante* (Little Traveling Cabaret), a live set recorded in Mexico City and released in the year 2000.

Recommended

Pequeño (1999)
Pequeño cabaret ambulante (2000)
El viaje a ninguna parte (2004)

Andrés Calamaro

An Argentine singer/songwriter with a complete disregard for the conventions of the music business, Andrés Calamaro is one of the most adventurous artists currently working the Latin rock field.

He began his career with Los Abuelos de la Nada—a group that also included notable musicians such as future record producer Cachorro López and Daniel Melingo. Calamaro would contribute memorable songs to Los Abuelos, such as "Mil horas" (A Thousand Hours) and "Costumbres argentinas" (Argentine Traditions). His first solo outing, *Hotel Calamaro*, came out in 1984 while he was still with Los Abuelos. Subsequently, he moved to Spain, where he formed Los Rodríguez, a successful outift that enjoyed singles such as "Mi enfermedad" (My Disease) and the smoldering "Copa rota" (Broken Glass).

Returning to a prolific solo career, Calamaro released the corrosive *Alta suciedad* (High Filthiness) in 1997. Two years later, *Honestidad brutal* (Brutal Honesty) was a stylistic tour de force, released in Spain as a thirty-seven-song double album. An abridged version with twelve cuts was released in the United States.

Honestidad is based on Calamaro's motto: "honesty is not a virtue but an obligation." With that in mind, he decided to write, rehearse, and record each song within the same day, faithfully capturing the essence of the tunes as they were being created.

The project evolved with recording sessions held in Buenos Aires, Madrid, and New York. In the end, Calamaro ended up with more than one hundred songs. From the opening track, "El día de la mujer mundial" (The Day of the International Woman), you can feel a unique voice surfacing among the fuzzy guitars and heavy 4/4 drums. Calamaro talks about driving through the countryside with a friend, smoking a joint, listening to the radio, and thinking about a woman he has left behind. The song evokes the pure rock poetry of Bob Dylan or Bruce Springsteen.

Other tunes include the bouncy "Maradona," which even includes a spoken interlude by the famous soccer player; the tango "Jugar con fuego" (Playing with Fire), with celebrated composer Mariano Mores on the piano; and the romantic "Paloma" (Dove), the kind of crunchy power ballad *rock en español* should revisit more often.

The year 2000 found Calamaro taking his most openly anarchic step by releasing *El salmón* (The Salmon), a quintuple album with 103 songs on it—a monumental work that's as mesmerizing as it is infuriating, a maddening mixture of gorgeous tunes and chaotic throwaways. It was clear that Calamaro didn't have commerce on his mind. He stopped touring, denied requests for interviews, and divided his time between Spain and his native Argentina, obsessed by the process of recording more and more songs.

Delving into this ambitious, fascinating work offers a glimpse into the soul of an artist who appears to be intent in minimizing the distance between music maker and listener, rock star and fan. Surrounded by a choice group of collaborators, Calamaro places you in the middle of his rehearsing space, pushing the RECORD button every time he feels he has something to say.

Often enough, he does. When he rocks, Calamaro sounds like a Latino Lou Reed, as in "Output–Input," with its mordant lyrics about S&M, drag queens, and Big Macs. When he goes pop, he sounds like a composer of advertising jingles on an alcoholic binge, satirizing himself and our shallow need for hummable ditties. There are also moments of punk, reggae, blues, eighties new wave, love poems, and obscene rhymes.

It is the softer side of Calamaro, however, that wins the day. There's some dreamy moments in *El salmón*, like the elegiac "Gaviotas" (Seagulls) and the smoky "Para seguir" (In Order to Carry On). Both of these make it easy to imagine the artist sitting by the piano, accompanied by the velvety sound of a muted trumpet, intoxicated by the powers of his creativity, saddened by the likable futility of the artistic process *per se*.

Not all 103 songs in the set are Calamaro's. He sprinkles his own compositions with a healthy dose of erratic numbers, from a handful of Lennon/McCartney classics (his version of "The Long and Winding Road" is particularly nostalgic) to the Velvet Underground's "Cocaine," the Stones' "Under My Thumb," as well as a number of classic tangos. The latter he interprets in true tango fashion, his gruffy voice spitting out the words with hate, mirroring the genre's morbid fascination with bitterness and defeat.

At the end of the fifth disc, Calamaro delivers a bluesy tune entitled "Este es el final de mi carrera." "This is the end of my career," he says. Commercially speaking, he might have been right.

Since finishing *El salmón*, Calamaro has reportedly recorded over two hundred new songs, planning to release them at one point or another. In 2004, he suprised his followers with *El cantante* (The Singer), a smoky—and somewhat uneven—collection of fascinating covers, including a tragic reading of the title track, the Rubén Blades–penned salsa song turned into a tragic anthem of Afro-Caribbean music by the late Puerto Rican singer Héctor Lavoé.

Recommended

Nadie sale vivo de aquí (1990)
Alta suciedad (1997)
Honestidad brutal (1999)
El salmón (2000)

Control Machete

There is an intensity to the darkly hued recordings of Monterrey-based Control Machete that makes them stand out from the other *rap en español* groups. Control began as a trio with talented producer Toy Hernández and rappers Pato and Fermín. The latter's raspy voice was the most recognizable element behind hit singles such as "Comprendes Mendes" (Do You Understand, Mendes) and "Sí señor" (Yes, Sir). Live, the group failed to evoke the urgency of its first album, relying on the more conventional elements of mainstream rap. Following the release of *Artillería pesada* (Heavy Artillery), Control was hit hard by the departure of Fermín, who left in order to launch an ultimately unsuccessful solo career as a Christian rapper. Toy and Pato carried on as a duo, inviting guests such as Mexican singer Natalia Lafourcade for their densely produced third album, *Uno, dos: bandera* (One, Two: Flag). The collection included a DVD with video clips illustrating each one of the CD's thirteen tracks.

Recommended

Mucho barato (1996)

Crucis

Progressive groups such as Genesis, Pink Floyd, and Yes were particularly successful among middle-class Argentinian youngsters during most of the seventies, inspiring a number of local groups to record their own concept albums with high-reaching fusions of rock, classical music, and traditional folk idioms. Crucis was the best of the bunch, largely thanks to the presence of Aníbal Kerpel—the future producing partner of Gustavo Santaolalla and an excellent keyboardist in his own right. Kerpel would contribute the atmospheric title track of the band's second and final album, *Los delirios del mariscal* (The Marshal's Delirium). Both *Los Delirios* and the band's self-titled debut were reissued on one CD during the nineties, and are recommended to discriminating prog-rock fans with a taste for the obscure. In the nineties, an Argentine impresario attempted to reunite Crucis for a massive nostalgia concert, but Kerpel turned the offer down, alleging that he was not interested in reliving the past.

Recommended

Los delirios del mariscal (1977)

Divididos

Following the death of Sumo singer Luca Prodan, guitarist Ricardo Mollo and bassist Diego Arnedo changed musical directions with Divididos, a power trio known for its heavy tendencies and reinvention of traditional folkloric tunes from Argentina. Success arrived in 1993 with the Gustavo Santaolalla–produced *La era de la boludez* (The Era of Dumbness). Divididos has changed drummers a number of times during its fifteen years of activity, but the group has remained consistent in its never-ending desire to rock hard.

Recommended

La era de la boludez (1993)
Gol de mujer (1998)
Vivo acá (2003)

Los Enanitos Verdes

Los Enanitos Verdes is a harmless pop-rock group from the Mendoza province of Argentina. Los Enanitos Verdes (The Green Dwarves) have transcended the poppy nature of their material by remaining true to their fans, recording a good dozen albums of original material, and infusing their many ballads with interesting guitar textures. They have been extremely successful on the strength of massive hits such as "Lamento boliviano" (Bolivian Lament) and a remake of the irresistible oldie "El extraño del pelo largo" (Long-Haired Stranger). Most of the band's material is merely adequate, but Los Enanitos can also surprise you when you least expect them to. *Guerra gaucha* (Gaucho War), released in 1996, was unusually moody and somber, whereas "Francés limón" (Lemon French), the opening track of their 2002 opus *Amores lejanos* (Distant Loves), is a peerless pop song paying tribute to French icon Edith Piaf.

Recommended

Guerra gaucha (1996)
Planetario (1997)

Fruko y sus Tesos

Fruko y sus Tesos is a tropical supergroup from Colombia whose seventies output provides a missing link of sorts between the seemingly disparate worlds of salsa and *rock en español*.

Salsa is a *de rigueur* genre for Latin rock fans in search of potent emotions. The parallels between the styles are many: the feverish intensity of the music, the emphasis on the sensuality of rhythm, the streetwise cosmovision, the concept of the live performance as a communal ritual, and the predominance of self-destructive performers—from Héctor Lavoé and Frankie Ruiz to Beny Moré and Fruko's own Joe Arroyo. Salsa is not a musical style per se, but rather an umbrella term used to describe a variety of Cuban-based dance formats (*cha cha cha, guaracha, guaguancó*, etc.) and their fusion with big band punch and R&B grittiness that took place in New York City during the late sixties and early seventies. From then on, the urban salsa sound spread successfully to Puerto Rico, Cuba, and other Latin countries, where it continues to flourish to this day.

Fruko y sus Tesos was created in the early seventies by venerable Colombian label Discos Fuentes—think the Motown of salsa. Striving to imitate the hardcore sound that was the rage in New York City at the time, producer Mario "Pachanga" Rincón and multi-instrumentalist Julio Ernesto Estrada ("Fruko") began consciously imitating Nuyorican salsa. But they couldn't help injecting a number of other influences into the mix: the softer melodic sense inherent in South American folklore and a certain psychedelic vibe that dominated mainstream pop-rock at the time, from the Beatles and the Stones to the Moody Blues.

Besides boasting a leader of unerring commercial instincts in Fruko, the band was lucky enough to enlist jazz pianist Hernán Gutiérrez, as well as three visionary singers: Joe Arroyo, Wilson "Saoko" Manyoma, and Piper "Pimienta" Díaz. Piper was an eccentric, wiry vocalist with a distinctly nasal pitch. His biggest moment with Fruko was "A la memoria del muerto" (In Remembrance of the Dead), a raw celebration of life over death. Saoko's chocolaty vocals provided some of the group's biggest hits: "El preso," the lament of the title's convict, and evocative vignettes from the Colombian *barrios* such as "El patillero" and "Los charcos" (The Puddles).

Arroyo, who had started his professional career at age ten singing in the whorehouses of his native Cartagena and joined the group while still a teenager, was Fruko's biggest discovery—a singer/songwriter whose appetite for excess has by all accounts proven to be almost as big as his protean talent. As a vocalist, he could switch octaves in a nanosecond, using the instrumental passages to generate a shrill, horse-like cry with his throat that quickly became his infamous battle call.

It was thanks to Arroyo that Fruko transcended the stylistic limitations of salsa, churning hits by the dozens while developing an explosive musical cocktail that offered tantalizing echoes of Bob Marley, James Brown, and Cuban *rumba*. His earlier sides with the group are especially recommended for their manic urgency and acid sensibility: "La cara del payaso" (Clown's Face) with its left field doo-wop harmonies; "Flores silvestres" (Wild Flowers) and its jarring, electric ending; and the reckless "Confundido" (Confused) blessed with an instrumental break that sounds right out of a James Brown funkathon. Arroyo was also a sensitive songwriter, turning the bitter experience of seeing a girlfriend drown during a beach outing into "Catalina del mar" (Catalina of the Sea). Like most Arroyo anthems, it was joyful and heart shattering at the same time, life affirming while also seeped in bitterness and regret.

Arroyo left Fruko in the early eighties to launch a solo career with his own group, La Verdad (The Truth). He survived an apparent drug overdose and became even more popular thanks to a string of hits and unforgettable live performances. At this point, the vague connection with Latin rock psychedelia is lost, as Arroyo turned for inspiration to other Caribbean formats such as soca and *compas*. To this day, Bob Marley remains his biggest musical influence.

Bridging the gap between pop, rock, and salsa, Colombian singer Juanes conquered the mainstream in the year 2000 with *Fíjate bien*, an album that includes an electrifying—and surprisingly faithful—cover of "La Noche" (The Night), one of Arroyo's anthems.

Recommended

Fruko y sus Tesos: *El preso—Greatest Hits 1* (1999)
Fruko y sus Tesos: *Grandes éxitos de salsa vol. 2* (1999)

Charly García

A certified eccentric, García has been one of the pillars of Argentine rock since its very inception. In the early seventies, Sui Géneris emerged as one of the genre's first supergroups, flirting with symphonic rock and confirming García's songwriting skills on naively arranged but undeniably melodious numbers such as "Confesiones de invierno" (Winter Confessions) and "Rasguña Las Piedras" (Scratch the Stones). Between 1972 and 1974, Sui Géneris released three studio albums, then bid farewell to its many fans with a massive concert at Buenos Aires' Luna Park that was recorded for posterity on the two-disc set and accompanying movie *Adiós Sui Géneris*.

García then formed the more openly progressive La Máquina de Hacer Pájaros (The Bird-Making Machine), which mocked the emergence of punk-rock and released two albums before breaking up. In 1978, Serú Girán combined García's prog-rock tendencies with a jazzier sound. The quartet included David Lebón, Oscar Moro, and a young Pedro Aznar.

The singer went solo in the early eighties, tailoring his keyboard playing and carefully calibrated sonics to express the unavoidable influence that new wave groups such as Simple Minds and the Cure had on him. *Clics modernos* is a well respected but strangely flat album from this period. Equally erratic on- and offstage (he has experienced troubles with the law for indecent exposure), García continues recording and touring to this day.

Recommended

Sui Géneris: *Confesiones de invierno* (1973)
La Máquina de Hacer Pájaros: *La máquina de hacer pájaros* (1976)
Serú Girán: *La grasa de las capitales* (1979)
Charly García: *Clics modernos* (1983)
Charly García: *Filosofía barata y zapatos de goma* (1990)

Ely Guerra

Ely Guerra is an immensely talented singer/songwriter from Mexico whose unorthodox recordings have yet to be rewarded with the kind of massive commercial success that she deserves. Guerra showed that she was a force to be reckoned with on her third album, 1999's *Lotofire*. The album's

passionate feelings and confessional poetry pull you into her conflicted world. With its eccentric touches of farfisa organ and liquid electronic beats, the excellent production by Venezuela's Andrés Levín underscores the singer's wounded voice.

An openly flirty Guerra returned sporting an Afro in 2004 with the double collection *Sweet & Sour, Hot y Spicy*. The opening track "Te Amo, I Love You" was a scorching rock anthem that hinted at the vocalist's desire to conquer both Latin and American markets. The collection was released as a single CD in the United States and, sadly, failed to generate much notice. Within the *rock en español* circuit, Guerra is venerated as one of the few female vocalists with an undying commitment to her art.

Recommended

Lotofire (1999)

Sweet & Sour, Hot y Spicy (2004)

Hip Hop Hoodios

An eclectic music geek with a passion for hip-hop and power-pop, Josh Norek developed a taste for Latin rock while working for a record label in Argentina during the midnineties. Back in the United States, he worked as a publicist, entertainment lawyer, and part-time music writer. Eventually, he summed up the courage to fulfill his fantasy of creating the first ever Jewish Latino hip-hop collective, accompanied by longtime friend Abe Velez and a coterie of prestigious Latin alternative musicians. The concept began as a joke (or did it?) with a self-released EP containing unforgettable nuggets such as "Kike on the Mic" and "Dicks & Noses," which showcased Norek's ease for concocting delirious rhymes and funky sound collages. By the time Hoodios released its full-length album *Agua pa'la gente* in 2005, the group was selling out venues in New York, Los Angeles, and Paris on the strength of more-conventional songwriting such as the melancholy "Gorrito Cósmico." Norek, who has always insisted that Hoodios is nothing more than "a part-time hobby" for him, threatened to retire from touring in 2006. It is hoped that the group's many fans will convince him otherwise.

Recommended

Agua pa'la gente (2005).

Illya Kuryaki and the Valderramas

The consistently infuriating but occasionally brilliant rap duo, Illya Kuryaki and the Valderramas, was created by two Buenos Aires teens—Luis Alberto Spinetta's son Dante Spinetta and Emmanuel Horvilleur. Obsessed with the pop culture clichés of foreign countries, Spinetta and Horvilleur mutate the American rap lexicon into Spanish, incorporating at the same time endless references to karate movies, Chicano slang, and Jennifer Lopez. *Chaco*—its name a reference to the Argentine province still inhabited by indigenous people—was a distinctive statement by two precocious (and excessively self-important) music makers. *Versus* was Illya's apex, a self-described "box of dreams" that began with the epic "Expedición a Klama Hama," complete with a majestic string section, eerie bells, and sensuous female choruses. "Demolición" was an authentic funk-metal workout, whereas the rest of the album found the pair exploring the sticky terrain of Prince-like erotic balladry. But *Versus* was a commercial disappointment and the duo's artistic dreams were somewhat crushed by the realities of the music industry. After the tragic death of manager José Luis Miceli in a car accident, Illya called it quits in 2001, with both Spinetta and Horvilleur remaining friends and following separate solo careers.

Recommended
Versus (1999)

Kevin Johansen

One of the most original Latin voices of the new millenium, Kevin Johansen was born in Alaska but grew up in Argentina.

Not surprisingly, his music is defined by an adventurous sense of multiculturalism. His elegant baritone and vivid imagination place him alongside quality artists such as Uruguay's Jorge Drexler and Argentina's Vicentico. Not coincidentally, both of them provide delightful guest spots on Johansen's 2004 tour-de-force *City Zen*.

The singer's second effort, 2001's *Sur o no sur*, was filled with snappy melodies and catchy combinations of mainstream pop and Latin genres. *City Zen* is even better. Johansen, who performs with equal ease in Spanish and English, has assimilated the countless sounds he heard traveling throughout the Americas—Brazilian samba, Argentine milonga, blues, South American folk, Beatles-esque harmonies—and reconstructed them through a sensibility that is culturally savvy but at the same time refuses to take itself too seriously.

City Zen is not a concept album, but the clash between a busy urban life and the search for the tranquility of a Zen-like void is a constant preoccupation throughout the record. Johansen announces the existence of an alleged "Buenos Aires Anti-Social Club," celebrates his friendship with tropicalia composer Tom Zé on the whimsical "Tom Zen," and expands on the "all is one" concept on the gorgeous "The Gem in I," one of the album's highlights.

Part of the fun in listening to the finished work is recognizing the rainbow of influences. The Beatles are all over the Drexler collaboration "No voy a ser yo" (I Won't Be Me— Johansen admits that the tune's chord structure is similar to "Eight Days a Week"). There's echoes of Sly and the Family Stone on "Atahualpa, You Funky!," a humorous tribute to the late folk pioneer Atahualpa Yupanqui. And at the end of "El palomo," he quotes "Cómo fue," one of Cuban crooner Beny Moré's most devastating boleros.

Johansen may be a cosmopolitan connoisseur of international music, but the record's deepest connections are intrinsically Argentine. The spirit of tango permeates the procedures, including a monologue by Tito, a professional taxi driver and part-time poet who recites a poem expressing his feelings of love and hate for the nicotine addiction that virtually destroyed his life.

The album's artwork reflects Johansen's love for Buenos Aires too. It depicts the singer sitting on the roof of the popular "number 60," a yellow bus that takes you from one extreme of the city to the other. Along the way, it stops in the heart of Palermo, the quaint barrio where Johansen now lives.

Recommended

City Zen (2004)

Los Lobos

Long before the mysterioso textures of *Kiko*, the avant-garde experiments of the Latin Playboys, or the polished revivalism of Los Super Seven, Los Lobos unplugged their electric guitars and spent years developing an acoustic repertoire of traditional Mexican songs.

Recorded in 1977, *Del este de Los Angeles (Just Another Band from East L.A.)* is a remarkably focused Spanish-only session that was originally sold as an LP at the band's gigs around East Los Angeles. The program is clearly designed to soothe the immigrant soul and his lacerating nostalgia for the homeland he left behind. Displaying the same eclecticism that would define their mature compositional years, the young Lobos were voracious listeners, hungry for any Latin song format rootsy enough to tickle their fancy. Enamored with the *son jarocho* from Veracruz, they replaced its original harp with mandolins, leaving the elegant flavor intact. *Rancheras* weren't a problem, either. "El pescado nadador" and "La feria de las flores" are the most effortless-sounding moments in this collection. Still, the musicians' reverence for the Latin American songbook doesn't get in the way of their playful sense of humor. Listening to raucous versions of "Cielito lindo" and "Guantanamera," you can almost see the mischievous grins with which they tackled these tourist favorites. And when it comes to bolero territory, Cesar Rosas' silvery crooning is deep and reverential. Even then, at a time when they played backyard parties for a case of beer, Los Lobos had the gift of making the most tired staples of Latin music sound hip again.

The rest is history, marked by their phenomenally successful revival of "La bamba," and memorable records such as 1988's *La pistola y el corazón*. The boys from East L.A. continue practicing their rootsy brand of rock 'n' roll tirelessly, providing inspiration to countless Latin rock bands such as Café Tacvba, Maldita Vecindad, and Ozomatli.

Recommended

Just Another Band from East L.A. (1978)
La pistola y el corazón (1988)
Kiko (1992)
Colossal Head (1996)

Miguel Mateos

Miguel Mateos is an Argentine singer/songwriter who reigned supreme in the eighties with his band Zas. When the group's self-titled debut came out in 1982, audiences were so shocked by Mateos' experiments with rock and funk *en español* that they thought the singer was actually doing Spanish versions of American hits. The band's live debut had taken place in 1981, opening for Queen in Buenos Aires in front of sixty thousand people. Legend has it that Mateos was so terrified that the show's MC had to push him onstage. Zas' subsequent albums, including the 1985 live collection *Rockas vivas*, sold hundreds of thousands of copies and made a rock idol out of Mateos.

Those glory days are mostly over for the singer, who went solo in the late eighties, moved to Los Angeles for four years, and has since returned to Argentina, where he has spent his time building a home studio and recording new material. Observing the deep socioeconomic problems that afflicted Argentina, Mateos started recording music that was darker and unlike anything he had ever done before. The result, 1995's *Pisanlov*, wasn't even released in his own country. Mateos returned three years later with *Bar imperio* (Imperial Bar), a tribute to the charms of pure pop and a futile attempt at returning to the epicenter of Latin rock. He also started working on a rock opera exploring heady subjects such as religion, metaphysics, and the passing of time.

Recommended

Zas: *Rockas vivas* (1985)

Nueva Trova

Nueva trova is a heavily politicized musical movement that blossomed in Cuba and South America during the sixties and seventies. The *nueva trova* artists believed strongly in the power of music to change the world. Some of their lyrics rank among the most beautiful poetry in the Spanish language. A musically omnivorous (and loosely connected) group of creators, they embraced folk, rock, pop, and jazz, creating an ambitious amalgam that often sounds like *rock en español* at its most introspective.

Although the *nueva trova* moniker could theoretically apply to artists as disparate (and seemingly unrelated) as Brazil's Milton Nascimento and Spain's Joan Manuel Serrat, its foremost exponents are Cuba's Silvio Rodríguez and Pablo Milanés, Argentina's Mercedes Sosa, and Chile's Victor Jara.

Silvio Rodríguez deserves a special mention here, since his influence can be felt on nearly all singer/songwriters from Latin America who began plying their trade after the seventies. Rodríguez is a one-of-a-kind artist whose extensive body of work should be explored by anyone interested in Latin music. His breakthrough album was 1975's *Días y flores* (Days and Flowers), a manifesto of leftist idealism and gorgeous melodies marked by its ability to turn words into powerful weapons of tenderness. Rodríguez has no equivalent in the Anglo world, although the works of Bob Dylan, Joni Mitchell, and John Lennon come immediately to mind.

Unlike the majority of *nueva trova* performers who remained close to their roots of mostly acoustic instruments and self-searching balladry, Rodríguez has shown a voracious appetite for experimentation in his forty-year career. In 1984, the three-part *Tríptico* celebrated the anniversary of the Cuban revolution with a symphonic cycle of songs that included romantic anthems such as "Nuestro Tema" (Our Theme). *Causas y azares* (Causes and Chances) flirted openly with jazz, whereas 2003's excellent *Cita con ángeles* (Date with Angels) found Silvio returning to his acoustic roots.

A number of *nueva trova* performers have, in turn, been seduced by the openness of *rock en español*. Mercedes Sosa collaborated with Fito Páez and recorded a stirring version of his "Vengo a entregar mi corazón" (I've Come to Deliver My Heart). Less daring than Silvio, Pablo Milanés favors a soft-rock approach that evokes a Cuban version of Sting.

Recommended

Silvio Rodríguez: *Días y flores* (1975)
Silvio Rodríguez: *Mujeres* (1978)
Silvio Rodríguez: *Rabo de nube* (1980)
Silvio Rodríguez: *Tríptico 1, 2, 3* (1984)
Pablo Milanés: *Antología* (1997)
Mercedes Sosa: *30 años* (1994)
Joan Manuel Serrat: *Mediterráneo* (1971)

El Otro Yo

El Otro Yo is the kind of group that you instantly love or hate the moment that you hear its music. With its thorny, guitar-based rock, low-fi anthems and indie attitude, the band sounds like the Latin rock answer to Sonic Youth.

Formed in 1993 by brother and sister Humberto Cristian Aldana and María Fernanda Aldana, the band has since its inception expressed a healthy disregard for commercial conventions. One of their early records is notorious for having been recorded in its entirety inside a small car. In 1997, the then trio caused quite a stir by releasing a triple CD with seventy songs, *Esencia—El Otro Yo del Otro Yo* (Essence—The Other Me of The Other Me), meant to showcase each one of its members' distinct personality on a separate disc.

The group's punk-friendly, DIY philosophy can sometimes give way to material that borders on the childish. Those occasional lapses, however, cannot obscure the remarkable instrumental proficiency of the band's members. Based on the lacerating guitar excursions of Cristian and the angelic background vocals of María Fernanda, 1999's *Abrecaminos* (Road Opener—with the band performing as a quartet with the inclusion of Ezequiel Araujo) switches effortlessly from quirky pop riffs to jarring passages of dissonance. Highlights from that album include the infectious punk hymn "No me importa morir" (I Don't Mind Dying) and the shimmering, poetic "Filadelfia."

Recommended

Abrecaminos (1999)

Ozomatli

Ozomatli is a gloriously multicultural combo from Los Angeles whose recorded output (three albums, one EP, and counting) has so far failed to capture the sheer exhilaration of its concerts. Song structure is not Ozomatli's forte, which explains why its live shows—based on funky improvisation and a dizzying parade of musical styles—showcase the collective at its very best. The band creates an imaginary bridge that unites the world of hip-hop and rap with a rainbow of Latin dance formats, from Colombian cumbia and Puerto Rican *bomba* to old-fashioned salsa and Brazilian-styled *batucada* drums.

Ozomatli's best effort, 2004's *Street Signs*, goes even further, incorporating Middle Eastern textures and guest spots by Nuyorican keyboard legend Eddie Palmieri and the Prague Symphony Orchestra. The resulting hybrid is undeniably invigorating, but it can also sound a bit unfocused at times. The group is respected for its extraordinary commitment to sociopolitical causes. A beloved ritual finds the band members finishing their shows by forming a samba line that crawls out of the venue and spills out into the streets, followed by their many fans.

Recommended

Street Signs (2004)

Plastilina Mosh

A pair of eccentric noisemakers whose influences range from Beck to the Beastie Boys as filtered through years of exposure to Mexican culture, Alejandro Rosso and Jonás of Plastilina Mosh anchor their musical activities to their irreverent attitude. This fact alone explains why the duo's 1998 debut album is a bit of a disappointment—a lot of hype but not enough substance.

Touring to promote *Aquamosh*, the duo stood on stage, a frozen smile on their faces, accompanying their monotonous, prerecorded rhythms with rudimentary bits of keyboards and guitar. The message was quite clear: Plastilina Mosh was one big prank, and the joke was on the audience.

Their second album, *Juan Manuel*, paints a strikingly different picture. The textures have become more abstract, the upbeat moments more fleshy and intense, and the contrast between aggressive party vibe and lounge inflection is now dramatic and thought provoking. Although conscious of its roots, the Mosh guys do strive to reproduce what the Latin sensibility may have sounded like to the American mainstream many decades ago. Their aesthetic resurrects the exported *cha cha cha* craze—with a couple of broken-down drum machines haphazardly thrown on top. *Hola chicuelos*, released in 2003, marked a return of sorts to the shenanigans of *Aquamosh* with songs such as "Cosmic Lelos," "Pinche Stereo Band," and "Shake Your Pubis."

Recommended

Juan Manuel (2000)

Reggaetón

Reggaetón is a decidedly crass but undeniably infectious movement that took over the landscape of Latin music between 2004 and 2005.

Born out of a spontaneous musical dialogue between Panama and Puerto Rico, *reggaetón* is the fusion of Spanish reggae, Latin hip-hop, and Jamaican dancehall. It was quickly embraced by Hispanic youth in both the United States and Latin America. *Reggaetón*'s ubiquitous anthem—Daddy Yankee's hyperkinetic, double-entendre-filled "Gasolina"—motivated millions of couples to shake their bodies in wild abandon as they practiced the suggestive *perreo* ("doggy style"), the movement's own dance.

Other *reggaetón* stars are powerhouse diva Ivy Queen, production team Lunytunes (they were at the helm of "Gasolina"), and the vocally impressive Don Omar. Standing slightly removed from his fellow artists but still very much a part of the *reggaetón* invasion, Puerto Rico's Tego Calderón is probably the genre's most inventive performer. His 2004 album *El Enemy de los Wasíbiri* includes nods to traditional Puerto Rican formats such as salsa and *bomba*. There's a psychedelic tinge to Calderón's records that adds depth to the expected *reggaetón* beats.

"I'm not really sure if I'm a *reggaetón* artist, even though I'm classified as such," Calderón observed. "I think of my records as Caribbean music. My style comes naturally to me because I just include all the different styles that I enjoy listening to myself."

The birth of *reggaetón* happened sometime in the early nineties, when Panama's El General and Puerto Rican rapper Vico C decided to transpose hip-hop to a distinctly Latin American sensibility. They found direct inspiration in the efforts of Panamanian vocalists who were dabbling with a local version of reggae.

At the same time, artists such as Yankee and Ivy Queen began to incorporate a dizzying variety of Latin folk elements into their recordings. Suddenly, *reggaetón* was quoting liberally from the Dominican Republic's merengue and bachata, Colombia's cumbia and *vallenato*, and Puerto Rico's own salsa and *plena*. Yankee went so far as to incorporate a *ranchera*-style brass section in some of his songs as a nod to his Mexican fans.

The strategy paid off handsomely. Latino fans from all origins found something to like in the new genre—and ambitious artists such as Calderón (a self-professed fanatic of iconic salsa singer Ismael Rivera) saw that *reggaetón* provided space for experimentation.

Genre detractors have plenty to complain about: the mind-numbing sameness of its bouncy rhythm, the sleazy lyrical content, and predictable rhymes. Because the Spanish language is rich and flavorful by nature, these qualities pose a challenge to MCs. Dusting up those dictionaries and studying Castilian poetry could easily result in tongue-twisting rhymes that have something to say. Considering that the movement has already experienced such tremendous success, most artists agree that an ambitious wave of artistic experimentation may be slow to come.

Recommended

Tego Calderón: *El enemy de los Wasíbiri* (2004)
Daddy Yankee: *Barrio fino* (2004)

Carlos Santana

Few musicians in the history of rock 'n' roll have championed the sounds of Latin America with the energy and consistency of Carlos Santana. By blending the soulful melancholy of the blues with the relentless fire of Afro-Caribbean tropical jams, this Mexican guitarist who grew up in Tijuana and spent most of his life in the United States created an entire rock subgenre that has served as a constant point of reference for countless musicians during the last three decades.

Santana invariably surrounded himself with extraordinary percussionists of Hispanic origin, favoring a three-piece percussive attack of congas, *timbales*, and trap drums that has included virtuosos such as Orestes Vilató, Francisco Aguabella, and Armando Peraza. On the classic 1970 *Abraxas* album, he introduced the genius of the late Tito Puente to the American mainstream through an extremely respectful version of the maestro's "Oye Como Va."

When it was time to engineer a triumphant comeback with 1999's poppy *Supernatural*, Santana shared his blessings with his Mexican brothers, inviting Maná to perform with him on "Corazón Espinado."

Recommended

Abraxas (1970)
Santana III (1971)

Sargento García

Led by the wiry, hyperactive Bruno García, the French collective Sargento García has many points in common with both Fabulosos Cadillacs and Mano Negra. But unlike those seminal outfits, the García gang has a deeper understanding of the Cuban *rumba*, which adds an extra kick to its frolicky ska-reggae hybrids. In fact, some of the group's instrumental segments sound as traditional as something hardcore folk ensemble Los Muñequitos de Matanzas would play.

Lyrically, García pushes a highly politicized, pro-immigrant agenda of unity and tolerance. But just like Ruben Blades or Manu Chao before him, he uses the sheer danceability of his tropical stew in order to communicate these important messages, a decision that places him a few notches above most *rock en español* bands.

Recommended

Un poquito quemao' (1999)

Sidestepper

Think of Sidestepper's debut as the kind of vulnerable love letter a man might write to the object of his affection without ever expecting to receive anything in return. The man in ques-

tion is Richard Blair, British record producer and salsa afi-
cionado. The recipient is Colombia and its bewitching music
scene.

After producing a session with traditional *cumbia* diva
Totó La Momposina for Peter Gabriel's Real World label,
Blair stayed in Colombia for three years and came up with the
idea of Sidestepper, a sound collective that would combine the
South American nation's tropical roots with *drum+bass*.

Like a well-connected spy, Blair operates through the help
of some indispensable local contacts. Iván Benavides, formerly
the leader of Bloque, brings his notoriously eclectic vision as
a cowriter to most of the tunes. Aterciopelados' Andrea
Echeverri adds her vocal sorcery to the bewitching "Linda
manigua" (Pretty Bushes). On "Me muero" (I'm Dying), Sidestepper turns to a Cuban *charanga*, complete with silky vio-
lins and acrobatic flute solos.

More than a revolutionary musical manifesto, Sidestepper
is a work in progress, which matured considerably on its second album, *3 A.M.: In Beats We Trust*. Both are highly recommended to Latintronica fans.

Recommended

More Grip (2000)
3 A.M.: In Beats We Trust (2003)

Luis Alberto Spinetta

Luis Alberto Spinetta is an iconic figure of Argentine rock—
a sensitive singer, guitarist, and songwriter whose unique
sound makes him instantly recognizable. Spinetta has been
one of Latin rock's most prolific names, working as a solo

artist as well as within the framework of several groups.
Unfortunately, he remains a virtual unknown outside of
Argentina.

Spinetta's first group was Almendra (Almond), a quartet
he formed with Emilio del Guercio on bass, Edelmiro Moli-
nari on guitar, and Rodolfo García on drums. Almendra's self-
titled debut remains, to this day, a classic on the strength of
strong, softly acoustic, and semi-psychedelic songs such as

"Las manos de Fermín" (Fermín's Hands) and the overwhelmingly haunting love song "Muchacha ojos de papel" (The Girl with the Paper Eyes).

Almendra's first incarnation (a second, less successful outing would take place in 1979) lasted only a couple of years. Spinetta expanded his horizons with Pescado Rabioso, yet another short-lived combo that favored a heavier sound and released seminal albums such as the double-LP set *Pescado 2* and 1973's ambitious *Artaud*. Then came Invisible, a trio that would later become a quartet, following a jazzier direction while showcasing Spinetta's trippy lyrics. The group's three albums are treasured by collectors and include 1975's *Durazno sangrando* (Bleeding Peach).

Spinetta's happiest moment as a bandleader came when he fronted the poetic jazz-rock collective Spinetta Jade. This group lasted from 1980 to 1984, and released a number of excellent records that, for the most part, have withstood the test of time. *Bajo Belgrano*, released in 1983, is a sweet, impressionistic album dedicated to the upper-middle-class Buenos Aires neighborhood where Spinetta grew up. Its "Resúmen porteño" (Buenos Aires Summary) is a poignant snapshot of Argentine reality during the difficult years of the military dictatorship. *Madre en años luz* (Mother In Light Years), released in 1984, includes "Ludmila," probably Spinetta's most evocative melody since "Muchacha ojos de papel."

Since the mid-eighties, Spinetta has released a solo album almost every year. He can be accused of a certain dryness in his sound, a repetitiveness that makes his recordings claustrophobic at times. That said, there's no denying the man's voracious creativity and discipline when it comes to writing and recording quality songs on a consistent basis.

Recommended

Almendra: *Almendra* (1970)
Spinetta Jade: *Bajo Belgrano* (1983)
Spinetta Jade: *Madre en años luz* (1984)
Luis Alberto Spinetta: *Pelusón of Milk* (1991)
Luis Alberto Spinetta: *Los ojos* (1999)

Sumo

Sumo is quite possibly the most criminally underrated outfit of the entire Latin rock movement. Sumo's brief existence from 1981 to 1987 changed the genre's aesthetic, making punk a viable proposition for Spanish rockers, incorporating reggae into the mix, and influencing everyone in its path with its heady combination of lyrical rage and the mercurial presence of vocalist Luca Prodan.

Prodan was an Italian who grew up in England and moved to Argentina in 1979 in a futile attempt to escape the heroin and alcohol addictions that plagued him most of his life. Other members included former music journalist Roberto Pettinato on sax, as well as guitarists Ricardo Mollo and Germán Daffunchio, bassist Diego Arnedo, and drummer Alberto "Superman" Troglio.

Sumo's songs reveal a variety of influences, from Bob Marley and Joy Division to the brainy soundscapes of Peter Hammill's obscure UK band Van Der Graaf Generator. Prodan's bilingual singing and occasional bits of proto-rapping are marked by his peculiar foreign-accented Spanish and his disarming sincerity. "La rubia tarada" (The Dumb Blonde) is the group's best tune—a vitriolic indictment of superficial Buenos Aires girls.

La rubia tarada, bronceada, aburrida
Me dice, por qué te pelaste
Y yo, por el asco que da tu sociedad
Por el pelo de hoy, ¿cuánto gastaste?

The dumb blonde, tanned, bored
She asks me, why did you shave your head?
And I tell her, because I'm disgusted with your
society
How much did you spend on today's hairstyle?

The steamy "T.V. caliente" (Hot Television) finds the singer fantasizing about Italian actress Virna Lisi while watching an old movie on television. An ominous crescendo of vocals and sax (a clear Van Der Graaf moment) provides a heated contrast to the peppy reggae verse that precedes it. "Los viejos vinagres" (The Old Farts) celebrates the folly of youth with an appropriately nimble beat and funky bass line.

Sumo's incendiary live shows quickly turned the group into a sensation within the local rock scene and the specialized press. But Prodan's alcohol binges continued and his health deteriorated rapidly. On December 22, 1987, the singer was found dead in his home. The remaining members of Sumo split the band into two different groups: Mollo and Arnedo created the folk-meets-heavy-metal trio of Divididos, whereas Troglio and Daffunchio continued as the party-friendly Las Pelotas. Both groups have been extremely successful, and wise enough not to tamper with the Sumo catalogue—thus enhancing and protecting the legacy of Prodan's group.

Sumo's music takes some getting used to, which explains its lack of appeal outside Argentina. It is particularly recommended to all those rock fans who are obsessed with seminal recordings from the sixties and seventies and who are looking for a "bridge" to the more contemporary sounds of the punk and new wave movement—and everything that followed them.

Recommended

Divididos por la felicidad (1985)
Llegando los monos (1986)
After chabón (1987)

Los Super Seven

You are likely to buy a plane ticket to the heart of Mexico when you hear what this loose collective of veteran musicians spearheaded by members of Los Lobos cooked up on their 1998 debut. David Hidalgo, Cesar Rosas, Freddy Fender, Joe Ely, and a few others team up with unusual synergy for a masterful revival record that looks into the future with unflinching optimism. Flaco Jimenez's sweet accordion haunts the record, just like the childhood memories of the musicians' parents listening to the radio marked them forever. The result is a session of hearty Mexican music that could only have been recorded in the United States. The inclusion of Woody Guthrie's "Deportee" adds to the overall feeling of racial solidarity and musical harmony.

Canto (Song), released in 2001, began with a gutsy move. Covering Ernesto Lecuona's "Siboney," one of Cuba's most revered classics, is the kind of challenge that separates the men from the boys. Los Seven's flawless rendition exudes the kind of solemn mood you would find in a religious ritual.

This nurturing feeling, the sensation that you are participating in a ceremony of sorts, is persistent throughout this excellent second album. Even when the group is partying hard, when you can almost see them smiling at the sheer infectiousness of Miguel Matamoros' salsa workout "El que siembra su maíz" (He Who Plants His Own Corn), *Canto* remains a serious record. Serious, because these musicians see the Latin American songbook as a source of spiritual renewal.

Eclectic and unexpected, the song selection is brilliant. In the hands of Los Seven, the cabaret poetry of Bola de Nieve coexists effortlessly with Caetano Veloso's tender *samba* and new compositions by Los Lobos' Cesar Rosas and David Hidalgo. The diverse background of the group's new members (Veloso himself, Peru's black diva Susana Baca, and the Mavericks' Raúl Malo) also hints at a new, pluralistic view on Latin music. Los Seven's first record looked at the future with optimism. On *Canto*, the dream has finally become a reality.

In 2005, *Heard It on the X* was a less sumptuous but equally effective exploration of border radio and the effect that it had on the musical lives of the Super Seven members.

Recommended

Los Super Seven (1998)
Canto (2001)

Los Teen Tops/Las Camisas Negras

Genre purists abhor the term *rock en español*. It's not rock in Spanish, they say. It's Latin American rock or Latin Alternative. Alternative to what? *Rock en español* began precisely as nothing more than that: rock 'n' roll, the original Anglo article, translated into Spanish.

Culturally speaking, Latin America has always suffered from an incurable inferiority complex. Whatever's hip in the developed world becomes dutifully imitated by the collective subconscious of the Latin countries. Musicians have spent the last six decades imitating and appropriating the styles of music that dominate the U.S. and British mainstream: from early rock 'n' roll and the Beatles to Dylan, the Stones, prog-rock, punk, the new wave movement, hip-hop, and electronica. At its best, Latin rock digested the influences and turned them into something new. (Tacvba's concoctions are arguably more interesting than the majority of music to come out of the United States in the nineties.)

During the genre's first two decades, however, transcending the influences was simply out of the question. Devoted imitation was the name of the game, and many of those early examples of *rock en español* are endearing today simply because of the candor and disarming sincerity of these attempts.

Enrique Guzmán's Los Teen Tops was one of the first groups to translate rock hits into the Spanish vernacular. Thus, "Good Golly, Miss Golly" became "La plaga" (The Plague), whereas "Long Tall Sally" was performed as "La larguirucha Sally" (this one sounds downright hilarious in Spanish), and "Jailhouse Rock" was played as "El rock de la cárcel." The Teen Tops burst on the local scene in 1960. They released five albums before Guzmán decided to go solo. His presence on the Latin scene influenced countless groups from Mexico, Argentina, and Spain into going rock.

Las Camisas Negras was another seminal group of the same kind. In their hands, "Blue Suede Shoes" became "Zapatos de ante azul." (The same tune would be covered fifteen years later by Argentina's rock pioneer Moris.)

There's warmth and good humor to be found in these recordings. They're gimmicky, of course, but there's a naiveté to them that would be understandably missing from later, better realized efforts in the genre.

Recommended

Los Teen Tops: *Los Teen Tops* (1960)
Las Camisas Negras: *Las Camisas Negras* (1959)

El Tri

The Rolling Stones of Mexico, led by the tireless Alejandro Lora, who spent most of the seventies and eighties exploring a psychedelic, rootsy blues-rock with cult outfit Three Souls in My Mind. Lora changed the band's name to El Tri and became the celebrated leader of Mexico's quintessential working-class rock outfit. His recipe is simple: a few crunchy chords on his guitar, the vertiginous fever of classic rock, and lyrics of defiance and rebellion performed vigorously with his trademark raspy voice. Lora is not an innovator but deserves respect for the zeal with which he continues to defend Mexico's unequivocal right to rock 'n' roll until the end of time.

Recommended

El Tri: *Simplemente* (1987)

Tributo a Héctor Lavoé

Tributo a Héctor Lavoé is an unreleased album that stands as a Holy Grail of sorts within the Latin rock discography. Spearheaded by longtime Latin rock manager and label owner

Tomás Cookman, the record pays tribute to salsa singer Héctor Lavoé and may be released soon now that Cookman has created his own label, Nacional Records. Lavoé, who died in 1993 at age forty-six, was one of the key figures of the Fania label, the New York–based record company responsible for the salsa explosion of the seventies. The vocalist's mercurial charisma, his disregard for conventions, and an addiction to heroin that ultimately destroyed his life bring to mind the persona of a rock star, which explains why so many members of Latin rock royalty responded enthusiastically to this tribute. Cookman envisioned the record as a bridge between the isolated worlds of rock and tropical music.

The album includes a version of "Calle luna, calle sol" (Moon Street, Sun Street) by Argentina's reggae outfit Los Pericos, with Lavoé sound-alike Domingo Quiñones on lead vocals. Ozomatli covers "Qué bien te ves" (You Look So Good) with _cuatro_ player Yomo Toro and flutist Johnny Pacheco, both of whom appeared in the original version. Veteran _sonero_ Cheo Feliciano goes rock on an impassioned "Todo tiene su final" (Everything Comes to an End) with Puerto Rico's La Secta. And Los Amigos Invisibles' Julio Briceño brings his _rico suave_ style of vocalizing to "Rompe Saragüey," performed as a restrained _cha cha cha_ by members of the Fania All Stars.

Known for its trashy funk permutations, the now defunct Argentine duo Illya Kuryaki and the Valderramas deliver an ingenious "Periódico de ayer" (Yesterday's Newspaper). Sampling a nostalgic instrumental passage of brass and strings from the original tune, MCs Dante Spinetta and Emmanuel Horvilleur rap about Lavoé's virtues and the fact that he is still alive in every Latino's heart. The duo has never sounded this soulful.

The project's most fascinating track is a heart-wrenching version of the Rubén Blades–penned Lavoé anthem "El cantante" (The Singer) as performed by Fabulosos Cadillacs with the addition of a string orchestra. The same song would be covered by Argentine rocker Andrés Calamaro on his covers collection *El cantante*.

The Lavoé tribute has been sitting on the shelves for years due to the dissolution of the RMM label, which was originally going to release it.

Vivencia

Argentina's Vivencia was the Latino equivalent of Simon and Garfunkel. The duo's folksy melodies, tender lyrics, and upper-class upbringing turned Vivencia into the laughingstock of the local rock community—a hardcore band they were definitely not. But their magnum opus, 1973's *Mi cuarto* (My Bedroom), has aged particularly well. A lovely album, it is seeped in a sweet, hippie-friendly vibe and includes memorable songs such as the melancholy "La mañana me reclama" (Morning Calls Me) and the wide-eyed innocence of "Los juguetes y los niños" (Children and Toys).

Recommended

Mi cuarto (1973)

Latin Rock: 100 Albums

1959
Las Camisas Negras: *Las Camisas Negras*

1960
Los Teen Tops: *Los Teen Tops*

1967
Los Gatos: *Los Gatos*

1968
Os Mutantes: *Os Mutantes*

1969
Los Shakers: *La conferencia secreta del Toto's Bar*

1970
Almendra: *Almendra*
Moris: *30 minutos de vida*

1971
Vox Dei: *La Biblia*

1972
Eduardo Mateo: *Mateo solo bien se lame*

1973
Sui Géneris: *Confesiones de invierno*
Vivencia: *Mi cuarto*
Moris: *Ciudad de guitarras callejeras*

1974
La Revolución de Emiliano Zapata: *La Revolución de Emiliano Zapata*

1975
Aquelarre: *Siesta*
Rita Lee: *Fruto proibido*

1976
León Gieco: *El fantasma de Canterville*

1977
Crucis: *Los delirios del mariscal*

1979
Serú Girán: *La grasa de las capitales*

1980
Three Souls in My Mind: *Bellas de noche*

1983
Charly García: *Clics modernos*
Spinetta Jade: *Bajo Belgrano*

1985
Pedro Aznar: *Contemplación*

1986
Titas: *Cabeca dinossauro*
Metrópoli: *Viaje al más acá*
Radio Futura: *La canción de Juan Perro*
Los Prisioneros: *Pateando piedras*

1987
Botellita de Jerez: *La venganza del hijo de Guacarock*
El Tri: *Simplemente*
Fito Páez: *Ciudad de pobres corazones*

1988
Síntesis: *Ancestros*

1989
Mano Negra: *Puta's Fever*
Os Paralamas do Sucesso: *Big Bang*

1990
Caifanes: *El diablito*

1991
Maldita Vecindad: *El circo*
Sumo: *Greatest Hits*
Luis Alberto Spinetta: *Pelusón of Milk*

1992
Fabulosos Cadillacs: *El león*
Soda Stereo: *Dynamo*
Gustavo Cerati/Daniel Melero: *Colores santos*

Fito Páez: *El amor después del amor*
Los Lobos: *Kiko*

1993
Gustavo Cerati: *Amor amarillo*
Divididos: *La era de la boludez*

1994
Café Tacvba: *Ré*
Mano Negra: *Casa Babylon*
Santa Sabina: *Símbolos*

1995
La Portuaria: *Huija*

1996
Café Tacvba: *Avalancha de éxitos*
Aterciopelados: *La pipa de la paz*
Soda Stereo: *Sueño stereo*
Jaguares: *El equilibrio de los jaguares*
Julieta Venegas: *Aquí*
Juana Molina: *Rara*

1997
Fabulosos Cadillacs: *Fabulosos calavera*
Molotov: *¿Dónde jugarán las niñas?*
Karnak: *Karnak*
Andrés Calamaro: *Alta suciedad*
Illya Kuryaki and the Valderramas: *Versus*

1998
Aterciopelados: *Caribe atómico*
Manu Chao: *Clandestino*
El Gran Silencio: *Libres y locos*
Gustavo Santaolalla: *Ronroco*
Los Amigos Invisibles: *The New Sound of the Venezuelan
    Gozadera*
Bloque: *Bloque*
Vico C: *Aquel que había muerto*
Carlinhos Brown: *Omelete Man*

1999
Fabulosos Cadillacs: *La marcha del golazo solitario*
Café Tacvba: *Revés/Yosoy*
Gustavo Cerati: *Bocanada*
Babasónicos: *Miami*
Enrique Bunbury: *Pequeño*
El Otro Yo: *Abrecaminos*
Ely Guerra: *Lotofire*
Sargento García: *Un poquito quemao'*

2000
Julieta Venegas: *Bueninvento*
Orishas: *A lo cubano*
Bersuit Vergarabat: *Hijos del culo*
Andrés Calamaro: *El salmón*
Sidestepper: *More Grip*

2001
Fabulosos Cadillacs: *Hola*
Fabulosos Cadillacs: *Chau*

Jaguares: *Cuando la sangre galopa*
Babasónicos: *Jessico*
El Gran Silencio: *Chúntaros Radio Poder*
Nortec Collective: *Tijuana Sessions, Vol. 1*
Gotan Project: *La revancha del tango*
Juana Molina: *Segundo*

2002
Vicentico: *Vicentico*
Orishas: *Emigrante*
La Mala Rodríguez: *Lujo ibérico*
Tribalistas: *Tribalistas*
La Vela Puerca: *De bichos y flores*

2003
Bajofondo Tango Club: *Bajofondo Tango Club*
Skank: *Cosmotron*

2004
Babasónicos: *Infame*
Los Amigos Invisibles: *The Venezuelan Zinga Son Vol. 1*
Bersuit Vergarabat: *La argentinidad al palo (lo que se es)*
Enrique Bunbury: *El viaje a ninguna parte*

2005
Liquits: *Jardín*
Natalia Lafourcade: *Casa*

Index